BUILDING YOUR EPIC LIFE

BUILDING YOUR EPIC LIFE

Your Journey, Your Way,
Your Masterpiece

LUCIANO CASTILLO

Purdue University Press
West Lafayette, Indiana

Cataloging-in-Publication Data are on file at the Library of Congress.

978-1-62671-209-6 (paperback)
978-1-62671-210-2 (epub)
978-1-62671-211-9 (epdf)

Cover image: Silhouette of a man and countryside under the stars and comets: m-gucci/iStock via Getty Images Plus

To My Son, My Daughters!
I feel such a deep love for you, and I will never
stop learning from you! I hope you build
your Beautiful Epic Life, and that I will be
fortunate enough to enjoy the ride with you!
and
My Parents
Their foundations of hard work, integrity,
and love in my early years made me
the man I am today. I love you!

The hero's journey is within you; tear off the veils and open the mystery of your being.

—JOSEPH CAMPBELL

Contents

Preface

We must believe that we are gifted for something,
and that this thing must be attained.
—MADAME MARIE CURIE

Our dreams can sometimes feel elusive, with physical or mental health challenges or simply the rigors of daily life that can keep us stuck in an unsatisfying place. In this book I am sharing with you how I played my game of life, from feeling negative or stuck, toward a beautiful, enriched life. This book is about creating a road map of your dreams and adding a deep purpose for your life—it is about helping you build your own Epic Life!

Most of us were educated in a system like a manufacturing plant, with little encouragement to think freely and creatively solve problems. The pressure to conform to the standards of others is a destructive source of stress to young men and women, which kills curiosity, and worse, it kills our passion.

I want to help you achieve a dream life that one day you will look at with pride because it is a life you designed, bravely pursued, and guarded. The examples of my own life are to share how I have become the person I am from persevering through a life that has been full of many challenges, failures, and successes, as well as one of hope.

Reading and engaging with me in this book could be one of the most creative endeavors you do—to design your own life. When you craft your own life over many years it will become a beautiful piece of art. This road map I am sharing with you is something I have done and perfected over many years. It is gleaned from many books, seminars, and my own life experiences. It worked for me and my mentees as a professor over many years.

Each chapter has a major quote by a historic figure to push forward the saga of the Epic Life, which is your own journey of becoming and discovery. At the end of each chapter there are activities for you to do. Please do not move forward reading the book until each activity is done. This is very similar to a typical textbook in the classroom. My goal is to help you build your blueprint for your life by acting and reflecting on the past, present, and future.

Also at the end of the book are some key recommendations of books, podcasts, art, and even movies that will help you refine your road map and put everything in perspective. Again, your road map will change over time, but you will be surprised about how much you are progressing over time. However, your life vision and purpose will be mostly set. I also created the activities at the end of the book to push you to become a lifelong learner. Thus, this is not your typical book you read on the weekend or in the classroom, and once you pass your course, in most cases you never review the material again. Instead, make it part of your life journey and it will help you overcome many challenges in life.

I hope that you enjoy this journey and that you build a beautiful piece of art that is your life—your Epic Life!

Acknowledgments

I am not a self-made man. I got a lot of help.
—ARNOLD SCHWARZENEGGER

I am so happy to be able to thank so many people who really contributed a lot to my life that culminated in this book, a book that I am so happy and proud we got done.

I always wanted to write a book that could change the lives of others—a book beyond my research and that could be used in classrooms to teach students to build a bold life—one that can change many lives and tell them, it is okay; breathe, you got this!

Believe it or not, I started writing this book during the Christmas break a few years ago (2023), when I was facing so much pain from another breakup. And for that I am thankful to her because it produced this book and many others! First, I need to thank my parents who taught me the values by which I live my life. I am deeply grateful to my mother, Carmen, and father, Luciano, "Chano" or "Otiano" as my grandparents called him, for their love, dedication, and examples they gave us for so many years.

My children have fueled my life with so much energy and meaning and yes, propelled me to be a better man so one day they can be better than me. I am so proud of each of you, and I can't wait to see how you build your Epic Lives. As I am about to submit this manuscript, I am so joyful about the birth of my first grandson. I can't wait to see him receiving the teachings and deep love from my son and daughter-in-law. I also want to thank my nephew Amil for reading the book carefully and giving me his great insights, and my cousins for their amazing support and feedback on the book: Sylvestre and JR.

Many of my students have been instrumental in building a method (e.g., Prof. Raul Cal, Dr. Jansen Newman, Dr. Gerardo Carbajal, Dr. Victor Maldonado, Dr. Tanya Purwar, among others) that works; if people apply it, they will see big-time results. Especially, thanks to my former student and friend Dr. Venkatesh Pulletikurthi for reading the manuscript and giving me his great suggestions. To my PhD student Andrés Castillo Jimenez for this great suggestion and remaking many of the graphs in the this book and the Spanish version. I also want to express my gratitude to Prof. William Serrano García from UPR-Humacao for reading carefully the manuscript.

Many of my friends—Latonia Jones, Crystal Madrid, Prof. Susan Tomizawa, Curtis Powell, Dawn George—thank you so much for your great insights and encouragement. My former wife Glenda Otero who always believed in me and for her unconditional love. Also, my good friends Prof. Arquimedes Ruiz-Columbie and Chancellor Dr. Miguel Velez for their positive view on life. And Maria Rindosova for the cover photo and fun discussions that led to the final chapter of the book.

I am also grateful to Purdue University for their support of this book, including Justin Race, Neal Novak, and many special thanks to Cristina Farmus. Also, my dear colleagues Prof. Jay Gore and Dean Arvind Raman who played pivotal roles in my moving to Purdue.

My editors, Lisa Solomon and Laura Williams, I am so deeply grateful for your dedication and patience over so many changes. In the end I am not self-made and so many people put their time and belief in me to do this book. And yes, we can turn lemons into not lemonade but gold!

My publisher for the edition in Spanish at Isla Negra, Prof. Carlos Gomez Beras who provided such great suggestions to ensure this book could be a valuable source for classrooms.

Thank you to God for giving me faith and hope, and so much energy to give my best every day, and for a journey called life and divinely guiding me and my family!

Thank you!

1

The Struggle Is Real

Introduction

> *Greatness is not achieved through comfort and*
> *complacency, but through overcoming challenges*
> *and pushing one's limits.*
> —ALEXANDER THE GREAT OF MACEDONIA

Most of us grow up in an education system that teaches rote memorization and what is needed to perform well on standardized tests or just meeting metrics. Grossly missing is the time to think freely and creatively, and encouragement to develop problem-solving skills and new ideas that emerge from your own curiosity. Individual expression and curiosity are undervalued in school systems that must hit high standardized test scores to keep their funding by reaching standardized minimum metrics of "success." The pressure to conform to others' standards can lead to students forgetting about and forgoing their passions. A passion of mine is encouraging free thought that helps people identify their passions and goals, then working with them to identify the steps necessary to reach these goals.

My name is Luciano. I work as an endowed chair professor of mechanical engineering at Purdue University. As a faculty member I conduct research on renewable energy and work with students to solve pressing problems in society. And, most importantly, I mentor my students to support them on their journey to be the best they can be, whether it be in research or as a classroom teacher. We also have fun together converting research problems into new technologies and patents. I have a fun career in which I am surrounded by young and smart individuals. This role allows me to see up close some of the pressing problems that many students and people throughout their careers experience due to stress and anxiety from a lack of direction or lack of fulfillment. The happiest moment for me as a professor is when I see my students graduating, standing tall and proud on graduation day, and see their parents beaming with pride.

On my way to achieving academic and professional success, there were times in my life during which I felt lost, felt as if I had no control of my life, even felt completely helpless as I watched people close to me struggle with physical and mental health issues for which I was unable to affect the outcome. Whether as a father or as a friend or as a professor, these situations were extremely taxing for me. In my professional career, I have seen graduate students cry many times from deep emotional stress. On a few occasions in my role as a professor (mentor), I worked with students that were on the brink of suicide. I'm proud to have mentored students on the more severe end of the autism spectrum. Figuring out how to support these individuals emotionally and academically as they started to build their own Epic Lives had a profound effect on me. I saw the importance of physical, mental, and spiritual health through helping my students in their own struggles while simultaneously dealing with my own. Through my experience, I developed a method to ensure I maintain a consistent daily routine that is shaped every day.

This book is a passion project for me. I find great fulfillment in helping others to find ways to achieve their full potential by helping them discover how to build a life for themselves on their terms, one that inspires them to take care of their physical and emotional health so they can triumph despite any challenges they may face.

My Journey: I started writing this book at the end of another year filled with ups and downs. The year had brought many challenges, including a divorce, which necessitated focusing even more on the emotional needs of my two teenage daughters and young adult son. But I was excited and pumped up about the coming new year. I asked myself, "Am I a better person today than I was last year? Am I doing better in my role as a father, friend, professor, and son?" I was able to answer to myself, *yes.* I have been creating my Epic Life for decades now, and my method gives me the strength to overcome difficult moments and stay focused on my goals and my values. An Epic Life is one in which an individual rises to the responsibility to become the best they can be, with joy and gratitude, to bring meaning to their lives and give their unique gift to this world.

Perhaps you are wondering why I consider myself qualified to write a book about building an "Epic Life." The answer is simple: I've failed. I've failed a lot, in many ways: professionally, personally, financially, and physically. But my "failures" weren't complete losses. I had learned so much from the seemingly "bad" experiences that I was confident that the coming year would be an epic year and knew with deep confidence that each coming year would be too—no matter what life would throw at me—because I had grown wiser and stronger.

> *Too many of us are not living our dreams because we*
> *are living our fears.*
> —LES BROWN

I have grown not only from surviving but from powering through challenges! You will likely feel similarly after you complete the activities in this book and execute your plans. I say this with confidence because "success is an inside job," something you create for yourself as you keep growing over time. I want to be clear here that creating an Epic Life is not about completing goals—it is about the person you become in the process. Goals are fundamental tools for growth. We will talk about how to use them skillfully—for their achievement and to reveal a new version of yourself over time. This is how you can move from routine and unfulfilling external measures of success to a truly extraordinary Epic Life.

A few years earlier, when I found myself in many "down" moments, I chose to turn these negative experiences to positives by calling them "bounce forward opportunities." I felt as if I'd hit the lowest possible point of my life. I had no idea there would be more equally trying times to come. Today I tell my children that failures, those painful, down moments provide big opportunities to grow as a person. You can build a better you when you use mistakes and negative experiences as springboards to build an Epic Life!

From these low points we can bounce forward to a better version of ourselves, build greater mental resilience, and contribute more to our world by staying in a mindset of learning, growth, and health, and pursuing those values that mean the most to us. If you keep learning from moments that didn't go your way, you can continually grow as a person.

Sadness, humiliation, and defeat are painful experiences. Yet, when you are brave and face these challenges, you can learn from them. At times you may feel as if you are stuck in a hole. Despite these feelings—in fact, because of these feelings—you can excel and build an epic year and future as you define it for yourself.

I want to share with you my life's struggles and the fulfilling life I've built in the hope my stories will inspire you to have the courage to follow your dreams and become a better you, even in the face of real obstacles and hardships. My journey from being a meek, fearful boy in Puerto Rico to a professor holding an endowed chair at a Big Ten university is a particularly long and unimaginable dream from that boy's perspective. I've dealt with homelessness and many years of abusing alcohol (at times to ease the pain of failures and at others to pretend I was happy) since I was 15 years of age, several divorces, painful break-ups, professional enemies, and a premature child at the brink of death several times. In this book I share with you a method I've developed and honed with dozens of students and others at major crossroads in their life: I call it a blueprint for achieving your Epic Life. Here you will find the tools you need to build your own Epic Life. The best is yet to come for me and for you!

Let this book inspire you to keep pursuing your dreams, to keep hope alive despite sadness or any rejections you might face. When you decide to look inward and love yourself, you can emerge stronger, feeling better about yourself, more peaceful, healthier, and happier than before!

In this book you will be shown a method to set goals in the form of a blueprint for your life that can help you "bounce forward" out of down moments toward an Epic Life, a life in which you are your own hero or heroine. I used this blueprint (you will create yours in chapters 7–10) along with goal setting and meditation to climb out of my lows and remain mentally and physically resilient. Now, I use it day after day and will do so throughout my life. A daily routine is best to achieve a resilient life. As you work through the activities in the book, you will devise a plan for yourself that will be a work in progress. Part of the recipe for success is recognizing what methods work best for you and adjusting your goals and blueprint to set yourself up as best as possible for success.

I will share books, authors, and learning opportunities that helped me, and at the end of each chapter there are activities for you to complete. By the time you complete chapter 10, you will have a detailed road map (e.g., goals, plan for execution, your values, your purpose in life and your vision, etc.) and skills you need to build your Epic Life.

Reading or listening to books, podcasts, pieces of art, biographies, or inspirational videos is not enough; one must take action toward building that life of your dreams. Whether you utilize one, two, or all the guidelines shared in this book, applying what you learn to your own life will facilitate your growth as a person. There are activities at the end of each chapter that will help you learn more about yourself and facilitate the process of building your Epic Life step-by-step.

I am here to tell you that by setting goals and letting go of thought patterns that do not serve you, you can be a better version of yourself—we must become experts at adapting and morphing to bring out our the best. Please, do not be afraid of failure—*failure is success in action*. Dedication is required to make lasting change. Take the steps needed to let the beautiful gifts inside of you come out and shine on the lives of others.

For example, when I was a PhD student, I was married to a woman who had three children—a major responsibility for a parent working on a PhD. As a graduate student I was paid a stipend intended to cover a student's modest living expenses, not to support a family with three children. I could have decided to quit my PhD program and used my bachelor's degree to find work as an engineer. But this was not my dream, so I worked harder than ever to support my family and study for a demanding but ultimately more rewarding career with more potential. My son, Khalil, was born, and my obligations grew even more—but so did my passion to finish my PhD, because I needed to provide my growing family a better life. My marriage was rocky and four young children at home is something very few students in their twenties handle. As I neared the completion of my PhD, my then-wife wanted to move all four kids to North Carolina to be close to family members. So, to help my family move and provide them financial stability, I chose to sleep on the floor of the wind tunnel of my PhD advisor's beautiful turbulence lab rather than pay rent. My commitment to fulfill my goal of finishing my PhD in mechanical engineering remained strong, but I realized the marriage was not meant to last. After a year of literally living in a wind tunnel, I became Dr. Luciano Castillo.

Later in my career, when I was up for a promotion to tenured professor (at universities, professors can earn a permanent position that allows them to pursue whatever scholarly work they choose), the process that can be so difficult and full of anxiety was relatively easy for me after the strength and wisdom I gained from navigating my family and financial life as a graduate student. I knew nothing was going to stop me from my dreams.

I will share with you how I made many of my tough decisions, from knowing when it is time to walk away from a dead-end relationship to adopting healthier behaviors. I had been drinking since I was 15 years young. Even though I stopped on a few occasions, I never made a serious commitment to put an end to my consumption of alcohol. However, in March 2024, one of my mentees was admitted into a stress center for a week, so I promised my youngest daughter that I would never drink alcohol ever again. To see someone I care about suffer so deeply was painful. When I learned that vaping exacerbated their condition, I realized it was an unfortunate real-life example that would be a powerful teaching moment for my daughters.

I used this as an opportunity to examine my own life. I thought about it and realized that my almost daily consumption of one to three glasses of wine could be detrimental to my health. I chose to stop drinking all alcohol, but also, I listened to several podcasts and read a few books on the detrimental impact of alcohol on mental health, and its long-term impact on the liver. For me, it was mind over matter. However, I know that for many, support groups and/or professional help is needed. If this is something you want to change in your life, the method I teach you can help you outline a plan.

Life brings pain. But when you acknowledge the pain, let yourself feel and face the pain instead of running away from it, you create an opportunity to move through it and become stronger. You can overcome it—pain has the seed for big-time growth; embrace challenges. This may require you to build a support system, ask for professional help, and take delivered action. You may need help; later we will talk about mentors, but for now, know that it is okay to get help so that you can overcome a difficult moment in your life. You can bounce forward to a better version of you, to have the best life, a life you once dreamed. It's not a sign of weakness to ask for help but the sign of a person that is brave. I talk later in this book about the people who helped me, and I hope this book helps you. And I hope you will recognize when others are struggling to build their Epic Lives and share what you have learned.

> *Your time is limited, so don't waste it living someone*
> *else's life. Don't be trapped by dogma—which is*
> *living with the results of other people's thinking.*
> —STEVE JOBS

Use the time you have on earth wisely and do something that will make you proud of yourself. It may take several iterations, but you can do it! After a particularly bad breakup I felt a very deep pain and sense of failure. But I took action to get better. I went to a Tony Robbins "Unleash the Power Within" event. I read as many books on relationships as I could find, and I thought carefully about how I could do things differently next time. Learning to select the best relationships for yourself is very important and will mark your life in many ways, and what we need can change throughout our lives. But better yet, I became a better me because I acted—a new version of Luciano! From that painful experience I learned so much about myself—why I made mistakes and had failed relationships that caused me so much suffering. Self-respect and self-love are an important part of living an Epic Life, and having a clear road map will give you the solid confidence that deep down in your heart, what you feel is what you want in this life, and you will know how to decide and act on it.

Each chapter of this book has a title representing the quality a person must have to achieve greatness in one or more areas of their life. Those who dare to pursue what at times could be a challenging journey—a journey of greatness—will be rewarded in many ways. While at times it may be lonely on that journey, your bravery will be noticed by people around you. I challenge you today to decide on what "Epic

Life" means for you. Then, do it, build it, fight for it! This is the single most important commitment of your life.

Why an Epic Life? The definition of "epic" as an adjective is "big, grandiose, extreme, or awesome," or, as a noun, it means "a long poem about the actions of great men and women or about a nation's history." For us, in this book, both definitions apply since the purpose is to create the best life you can build for yourself. And as you achieve the awesome life that you design, you become your own hero! Thus, taking the courage to build the Epic Life you deserve is indeed a heroic action you will take for yourself when you unlock the courage to build and act upon that dream life you once believed you could achieve.

Interests: By exploring different activities and being curious about different things in life, you learned some lessons and you decided this is not for me or you discovered a new passion. Your desire may vary at different stages of your life. For me, once I became a champion of Motocross in the 100 cc category when I was a teenager, I was ready to pursue my next big chapter—to be an engineer. Not just any engineer, an amazing engineer. How did I know I wanted to be an engineer? It was my dad, a man with a high school education and some courses in real estate. One day, I was with him driving to visit a customer, and as we drove close to the refinery, he asked me, "Kilo [my family nickname—why, I do not know], do you see that refinery there? All of that is designed and built by engineers, chemical engineers, and they solve problems!" That was all I needed to know, and I later went on to study mechanical engineering—a career that brought me so much joy and gratification. Later, we will talk about the importance of mentors. Friends, I didn't even know what an engineer does. All I knew is that "they solve problems" and they design stuff; as explained by my dad—one of my big-time mentors and heroes!

> *That's why the philosophers warn us not to be*
> *satisfied with mere learning, but to add practice and*

then training. For as time passes, we forget what we
learned and end up doing the opposite, and hold
opinions the opposite of what we should.
—EPICTETUS

CHAPTER SUMMARY

I want to welcome you with all my heart to this journey we're about to take together. In this first chapter, I open up and speak to you straight from the soul. I share my story—the highs, the lows, the heartbreaks, the moments I thought I wouldn't make it and how, despite it all, I kept rising with even greater strength. I've experienced failure in every form: personal, professional, financial, and emotional. I've felt lost, powerless, watching people I love suffer without being able to help. But I learned something powerful—every fall can become a launchpad if you choose to bounce forward.

As a shy kid growing up in Puerto Rico, I never imagined I'd one day be a tenured professor at a Big Ten university. But here I am—not because the path was easy, but because I chose to grow through what I went through. I slept on the floor of a wind tunnel, battled alcohol abuse, went through painful breakups, and watched my kids face their own dark moments. And through it all, I learned that living an Epic Life isn't about perfection—it's about becoming the best version of yourself, with joy, with gratitude, and with fire in your soul.

This chapter is both my testimony and my invitation to you. I want you to know that building a life filled with purpose, resilience, and meaning is absolutely possible. That dreams don't have deadlines. That you already have what it takes to be the hero of your own story. In this book, I share the method I developed alongside students and others at life's crossroads—a method that helped me stay grounded and focused, even in my darkest hours. Because success, my friend, is an inside job. And your journey starts now. And trust me—the best is still ahead!

CHAPTER ACTIVITIES

ACTIVITY #1. Your Story, Your Background

Time needed: Approximately 10–30 minutes. Materials needed: Journal dedicated to the exercises in this book and pen or pencil. The physical act of writing is important for analyzing and reflecting about your life. Look at your life up to this point.

Instructions: Answer the two questions below in your notebook devoted to building your Epic Life. This notebook will become your blueprint for building your Epic Life. I recommend a notebook because writing on paper can foster creativity and rewires your brain as your hands move. The slower, more deliberate process of handwriting allows your mind to wander, which can lead to new ideas and insights. If you do it on your phone instead, the fast pace of typing and the constant temptation of distractions from notifications can inhibit creative thinking.

1a. What is your story? How did you get here?
1b. What stands out in your story in terms of challenges or great moments?

RECOMMENDATIONS

Books

Man's Search for Meaning. Viktor E. Frankl. Herder Editorial, 2004. A profound reflection on how to find purpose even amid extreme suffering.

The Four Agreements. Don Miguel Ruiz. Urano, 1997. A Toltec wisdom manual that proposes principles for a fulfilling life free from unnecessary suffering.

When Things Fall Apart. Pema Chödrön. Editorial Oniro, 2006. A spiritual guide to embracing uncertainty with compassion and courage.

Biographies

Long Walk to Freedom. Nelson Mandela. Aguilar, 1995. The memoirs of Nelson Mandela that portray his struggle against apartheid and his philosophy of reconciliation.

Frida. Hayden Herrera. Bloomsbury Publishing, 1983. A portrait of the Mexican artist that shows her strength in the face of physical and emotional pain.

My Brief History. Stephen Hawking. Crítica, 2014. The inspiring story of Stephen Hawking and his scientific path despite a motor neuron disease.

Movies

The Pursuit of Happyness. Dir. Gabriele Muccino. Columbia Pictures, 2006. The true story of a father who fights against adversity to give his son a better future.

Life is Beautiful. Dir. Roberto Benigni. Miramax Films, 1997. A father uses humor and imagination to protect his son during the Holocaust.

Slumdog Millionaire. Dir. Danny Boyle. Fox Searchlight Pictures, 2008. A vision of how life experience and resilience opens the way to unexpected opportunities.

Works of Art

Guernica (1937), by Pablo Picasso. Museo Reina Sofía, Madrid. A protest against the violence of war and human suffering.

The Scream (1893), by Edvard Munch. National Gallery of Norway. A powerful representation of existential fear and internal anguish.

The Starry Night (1889), by Vincent van Gogh. MoMA, New York. Reflects Van Gogh's emotional turbulence and his quest for beauty amid chaos.

2

The Winner in You

Life Is Like a Video Game

You just can't beat the person who never gives up.
—BABE RUTH

Think about how you got here. On the biological side, you were a winner at the time of conception. Over forty million sperm fight to fertilize an egg first. You survived months during which several things could have gone wrong that could have ended the pregnancy. Your DNA fully expressed itself and got you out in the world as a winner! The sperm that created you was required to fight, overcome, and achieve to win its prize of fertilizing the egg and creating you—that makes you a big-time winner!

Biologically you have the genes of a winner, and you are destined for greatness! It's up to you to make the most of the opportunity afforded you to have a great life. Your job now is to figure out the unique gifts and passions you have and to allow them to flourish. By sharing your unique talent(s) with the world you can become world-class in something—but the process of becoming world-class in something that can be challenging. The problem is that even when you are born with all the tools needed for greatness, society often throws self-defeating, negative thoughts at us, leading to an "I can't" mentality. Sometimes, teachers, parents, grandparents, and friends say things that may unintentionally (or intentionally) contribute to a lowering of your self-esteem and self-confidence. These can create roadblocks on your life's journey.

Over the next pages, I will encourage and support you on how to reframe your "negative" stories to ones of greatness, ones in which you gained valuable experiences and learned important life lessons, even if you didn't realize it at the time. Despite failures, health challenges, injustices, bad breakups, or a divorce, you have a unique gift to share with the world. You owe it to yourself and society to find your gift, then polish it, groom it, expand it to a gift that you give away to others—so they find their own voice and then share it with the world. In the process of sharing and giving to another, you improve the world and become a better version of you. Sometimes you realize that you have many gifts or that Mother Nature wants you to grow more and polish that gift further. Some big challenges—or, as we call them, "problems"—may be thrown at you, and you may feel sad and be upset at how unlucky you feel you are in life because you lost a job, a loved one passed away, or you and your life partner decided to go your separate ways. In some cases, the challenge is not as extreme as these examples, but you take on the role of victim, you see it as someone else, an external force, doing it to you—the parent, the boss, the boyfriend or girlfriend—but if you think objectively and try to find the gift in those challenges, you can emerge as that new amazing person that you never imagined.

Each time life brings these unique moments of damage or pain, we receive signs that we are alive, and we have unlimited opportunities to grow and be better than before. For a physical example, in weightlifting, one achieves muscular growth by pushing to the point where small tears in the muscles appear, making room for new muscle tissue to fill in the cracks. Pushing past the limits of one's comfort zone is where growth happens. With weight training, we may get very sore as part of the process of getting stronger. By alternately pushing and resting, we grow! Well, in life we have happy moments when everything goes well according to our plans, and then we have moments that bring pain, difficulties, and even deep sadness. Rather than staying down and feeling defeated, get up and know that at that low moment in your life, if you dig deeper, learn from that experience, go out and learn about that issue with an open mind (e.g., relationships, health and fitness, finances, nutrition, etc.), there is an amazing opportunity for you to grow, to become better, to become more loving of self and others, richer, stronger physically, and wiser. Then, you can connect what you have gained from the difficulties in your life with your gift and understand who you truly are as a person—as a being. That, my friend, is a gift that you not only give to yourself, but also one you can then share with the world to make the lives of others better and yourself happier, wealthier, or simply a better version of you. Take what we call "negative" as motivation, even though it's uncomfortable or may seem so painful at times—remember failures are success in progress—take them as hidden treasures! Behind the challenges, there is a lesson for you to uncover and make it yours! You were born a winner, you overcame obstacles, you have the seed of greatness within you that you must grow.

In spite of all of your challenges, you decided to be here; you pushed hard to be here. Reading this book is an action you chose to take, a tool you are choosing to use, to support yourself in your journey to an Epic Life—knowing this now changes your attitude toward life. Now, fulfill your dream and uncover who you are. Evolve to a new you, shed the old skin, get up, and be the best you can be today. Do not be afraid of falling because when you fall, you can get up and try again to get stronger, and even jump farther than before. Dare to be you—the real you that is hiding deep inside of you; dare to be brave and fulfill your dreams, which emerged even before you were a sperm and egg—but this is a conversation for another day.

Right now, I want you to know that you have the power to be a winner, not just once, but many times over, and each time you get better the world gets better—approach each day with a positive attitude that today will be a better day. We are as one organism working together whether we want to believe it or not. Do not ever let negative voices, negative characters, or the bad wolf eat away your dream of greatness that is dormant within you. Be ready to explore new things to dare to let out the greatness hiding inside of you!

Video Games and Life: Think of yourself as a sun, a nuclear reactor with more than enough energy to power a community. Think how your gift(s) that you have kept hidden from yourself and others, if unleashed, would help so many lives in so many ways. For example, your jokes could bring happiness to others, or you could find a cure for cancer, or your gift of teaching could help a child blossom in math—imagine how that child's life could be transformed if your unique talent and patience helped someone in need. Imagine how your ideas could make soldiers with PTSD live a better life after they fight so that we can have freedom or helped children suffering from war, climate change, or poverty have a better life. By becoming amazing not only do you help yourself but the lives of others—this is adding value to society and thus translates to economic benefits to you.

When a person does not discover, ignite, and push forward with a gift that is inside of them, when they keep their gift(s) buried, hidden from themself and the world, they deprive so many people including themself as that gift could bring economic benefits. We owe it to ourselves and others to uncover that burning desire—it is that passion you feel inside of you for doing something you love or enjoy that is very important to you. Therefore, do something that makes us and our world a better place, then pursue it passionately—and share it with the world.

> *Riding a race bike is an art—a thing that you do*
> *because you feel something inside.*
> —VALENTINO ROSSI

So, each step in life you take, see it as helping you find some gifts— your treasures. By doing this, you now see your journey as a game of discovery. Sometimes, as in a video game, when you win a section and move to the next level, there are some new skills you need to develop, right? And you are rewarded with treasures or prizes along the way. Well, you lose to an opponent, or you kill a big dragon with a new trick you learned in the previous stage; and when you lose you get to come back and learn that skill, right? Well, this is how life is, my friends—life is a game of learning and discovery. And the more you win, the more you discover who you are, because each experience has a unique prize only for you. This is very personal, and the lesson varies from person to person. Unfortunately, when we win, we do not reflect on it; however, when things do not work out our way, we throw a tantrum or get depressed. Take a minute the next time you "lose" in this way. What unique lesson can you learn from this experience? Then, get up and play again, and continue until you learn to enjoy the process and can share with others some of the lessons or tricks you have learned. The game becomes even more fun when you see the paths of others and their process and progress! So, "failures" are those lessons we need to learn to keep playing the game of life; and, friends, "sharing those lessons with others" brings true fulfillment and joy into your life! Keep in mind that "failure" is success in action.

Using that burning desire, that passion to pursue something epic is critical, because it will set a big energy booster for you. Friends, you decide the type of game you will play—take the first step and do not be afraid of "failures"; that is how you learn to move up to the next level.

"Epic" is a relative term. Something that seems ordinary to you in the present may strike you as a unique or special gift at a later point in your life. The game you play is related to your gifts. Think of something you can spend hours on or something that seems to come so naturally and easily for you. Something you enjoy doing and can do for many hours. Think of that one thing you could do the rest of your life—even if you do not get paid! Do not worry if it pays well but think about how you could help others by doing that—the more solutions or value you bring to others, the bigger your reward. Later, I will show you how to leverage that gift. In other words, use your gift to solve problems for society—that is how I play my game!

The secret is that as you grow, you get good at some lessons (formal education or self-taught), gaining new knowledge and experiences— bringing joy into your life. By the time I was in my teens, I realized that I was good at solving problems, and I liked playing movies of my life and my future (e.g., daydreaming). When working in the family car business, we all needed to be creative problem solvers, because every customer had different issues. But I quickly learned to make connections between cars and problems that showed up. When employees were sick and did not show up, it created problems—but I learned to do it myself. We had to figure out how to fix the problems for our customers and thus increase the income for the family business. Your burning desire, regardless of your age, is there—just find it and use it to propel you forward. For me it was fun because at the end I had a reward—I will get paid, I will fix my motorcycles, and then I will go out and race.

Embrace and Be Grateful for Your Stage: Everyone in life has a unique beginning and end, and how far you go in your game of life depends on how well you embrace the beginning of your life. There is no way for you to change how you are born, where you are born, your parents, your race, the color of your skin, your height, and so on. If you approach your game of life with gratitude and be grateful for who you are, regardless of how good or bad your childhood was, the more you can focus on your path ahead in your life game. Nobody knows for sure how long we will be here, but our job is to live fully in the time we are given.

Steve Jobs was given up for adoption. He could have spent all of his life complaining and crying about why his mother gave him up; instead he embraced the love his adoptive parents gave him, and he created the information age—more than the iPhone or the Mac with Wosniak. Yes, he died relatively young at 56; yet he is considered one of the most consequential individuals of this era. There is another great man that I have a lot of respect for: Nick Vujicic, who was born without legs and arms, yet he built a full life in every way. The man was bullied in school and at some point, he wanted to kill himself, yet he raised himself from depression and became an inspirational speaker, a pastor, and has been happily married for many years; and yes, created wealth for himself and his family—this is a beautiful human being. I highly recommend his book *Life Without Limits*. In spite of his difficult beginning, he played his game of life with hope and optimism, and he touched so many lives.

My friends, whatever was your past, make the decision to play your game to the fullest. Embrace the people that come into your life, have the courage to be the best you can be, and start playing your game to the highest level. Learn to love yourself, your color, your gender, where you came from. Be the best you can be today, not tomorrow or one day— start living your amazing game today.

CHAPTER SUMMARY

Never take for granted that you are special, that biologically you have the genes of a winner, and you are destined for greatness! Your job is now to find what unique gifts and passions you have and to allow them to flourish so that you embody that talent and share it with the world. If only this process of becoming world-class were easy, but it is not and it takes overcoming and learning from many "failures."

Approach life as a video game—each stage has some lessons to learn, and "failures" are sprinkled throughout to help you gain knowledge and gain skills you need to jump to the next level of your game. You get to define your game of life! To expand your knowledge or get a sense of how you play your game, pay attention to those areas where you feel a burning desire, a strong passion, or just interest—here are the clues when you should move forward in life. Look for stories of achievement in movies and biographies of heroes and heroines that changed the world with their burning desire and see what caught your attention and what they did (e.g., see the recommendations at the end of the chapter). They made history because they were brave and pushed and pushed until they got to the finish line in their own personal game of life! Each of us has a different purpose in life and yours is unique because you, my friend, are unique. You do not have to play the same game of life as your parents, or what the media says you should play—it comes from within! I challenge you to have the courage to pursue greatness by pursuing your own game! And that saga of finding your gifts and developing them to become the best you can is The Epic of Your Life!

CHAPTER ACTIVITIES

ACTIVITY #2. Moments

Time needed: Approximately 10–30 minutes.

2a. What wins have you experienced in your life?

2b. Try to vividly remember those moments in detail. How did you feel? What senses were in play? What colors do you see? Who is there? What sounds or songs do you hear? What do you smell?

2c. Why is that experience important to you?

ACTIVITY #3. Joy

Time needed: Allow about 20 minutes for this activity.

3a. What brings you joy? Why?

3b. What activities do you enjoy doing that you can spend hours and hours doing?

3c. Write a list of 10–20 careers or businesses you could do to solve problems in society. How can you use your skills or activities you love to solve those problems?

RECOMMENDATIONS

Books

Mindset: The New Psychology of Success. Carol Dweck. Ballantine Books, 2006. Explains how adopting a growth mindset—instead of a fixed one—can transform your life. It teaches us that our abilities can be developed through effort, the right strategies, and continuous learning.

Grit: The Power of Passion and Perseverance. Angela Duckworth. Scribner, 2016. A powerful reminder that success depends not only on talent but on the combination of passion and perseverance over time, even in the face of failure.

Awaken the Giant Within. Tony Robbins. Free Press, 1991. This personal transformation book invites you to take control of your emotions, finances, body, and relationships to awaken your inner potential.

Jonathan Livingston Seagull. Richard Bach. Scribner, 2014. An inspiring fable about a seagull that refuses to live limited by what others expect of it. It's a call to follow our dreams and fly beyond self-imposed limits.

Mastery. Robert Greene. Viking, 2012. Explores how to achieve excellence through continuous learning, observation, and deliberate practice. Includes inspiring stories of geniuses like Leonardo da Vinci and Michael Faraday.

Think and Grow Rich. Napoleon Hill. Tarcher, revised edition, 2007. A classic on how focused thoughts and beliefs can create wealth. Based on interviews with the most successful entrepreneurs of the 20th century.

The Magic of Thinking Big. David J. Schwartz. Touchstone, 1987. Teaches how ambitious thoughts, self-belief, and decisive action can open doors to great achievements, both personal and professional.

Life Without Limits. Nick Vujicic. WaterBrook, 2012. The author, born without arms and legs, shares his inspiring story of faith, resilience, and purpose, proving that no barrier is insurmountable with self-love and determination.

Biographies

The Greatest: My Own Story. Muhammad Ali. Random House, 1975. The autobiography of Muhammad Ali, revealing his personal struggle inside and outside the ring.

My Life: Queen of the Court. Serena Williams. Simon & Schuster, 2009. An intimate account of the champion Serena Williams and the challenges she faced in her career.

Faster than Lightning: My Autobiography. Usain Bolt. HarperSport, 2013. From his humble childhood in Jamaica to becoming the fastest man in the world.

Movies

Rocky. Dir. John G. Avildsen. United Artists, 1976. The story of an unknown boxer who proves the value of perseverance.

Coach Carter. Dir. Thomas Carter. Paramount Pictures, 2005. A coach who demands academic excellence and character from his players.

Rudy. Dir. David Anspaugh. TriStar Pictures, 1993. A young man pursues his dream of playing football against all odds.

Works of Art

David (1501–1504), by Michelangelo. Galleria dell'Accademia, Florence. Represents bravery in the face of the impossible; a symbol of human courage.

Nike of Samothrace (ca. 190 BC), unknown artist. Louvre Museum, Paris. A classical sculpture that celebrates victory and triumphant effort.

Atlas Holding the Sky (classical mythology). Various historical representations. A mythological figure symbolizing the burden and responsibility of holding the world.

3

"FAILURES" = SUCCESS IN ACTION

I have not failed. I've just found 10,000 ways that won't work.

—THOMAS A. EDISON

The great Michael Jordan, the best basketball player of all time, missed 3,000 shots, including a three-pointer in a final game, and is still known as the greatest! Whenever someone is inducted into the Hall of Fame or awarded a Grammy or an Oscar, we hear how great that person is, how amazing—we might even think that he or she walks on water! What we don't see is how that individual persevered through multiple failures, time after time, and many times they faced tragedies—deep down, they will tell you, it was not easy. Nobody talks about those failures, either because of embarrassment or to keep the impression they are perfect; and yet without failing the person you see today would most likely not have been recognized as a superstar!

Muhammad Ali, the 1974 Sportsman of the Year, lost over and over and over, sometimes to inferior opponents, even one that broke his jaw. However, he was and still is nicknamed "the Greatest." He is unique—the only Muhammad Ali that existed. He stands out for his principles and his continuous fight for equality for Black people. He was very vocal in his fight and used honesty, humor, and even poetry. He did it his way, as only Ali could, and through all of this he remained and is remembered as a respected and admired leader.

I could tell you stories upon stories from almost any area or walk of life about failure and resiliency. As I write this book today, I think back about the numerous failures I have experienced, so many that I could write an entire series of books on my failures as a teen and another full series on my failures as an adult—yet I am so proud of the person I am today, not because of any achievements but because of the lives I was able to touch and who I am as a person. I will share with you some of the failures and explain how they led to important changes in my internal sense of myself. Today when I look in the mirror, I am proud to say, "Man, Luciano, I am so proud of who you became." If my life were to end today, I would feel happy and proud of the life I have built. But there have been plenty of losses and challenges along the way.

In 2023, I found myself getting divorced yet again, for the third time. However, learning what I did from the end of my first two marriages, my third wife and I started our marriage with the agreement that if it didn't work out, we would get an annulment. We quickly realized it wouldn't work out. A few months later, I managed to start yet another serious relationship.

This time I decided to take a harder look at my failed relationships. Was I repeating a pattern I had neglected to identify and correct? In doing so I realized that I had been compromising myself in ways that caused me to sacrifice things of importance to me—my freedom—and at times it was as if I fell into a relationship. My last relationship was with someone I felt deep love for and whom I considered special in many ways. I really wanted this relationship badly. However, for it to "work," it would be at an even greater cost, and yes, sometimes our own fears of failure make us run as I did in that relationship. Having pivoted from looking at my three previous marriages as failures to seeing them as opportunities for learning allowed me to better see what does and does not work for me in a relationship. That was me at 57.

That last breakup sent me to a live seminar with the great Tony Robbins to reboot myself. I was feeling deep pain from three, almost four failed marriages. During that time, each of my children was experiencing different versions of me. And I must admit that I was also causing others a lot of pain that they did not deserve, and perhaps if I were less afraid of being hurt again, my last relationship would have been amazing.

For example, I found myself receiving advice from my daughters, in part because I was doing everything I could to hide so much pain—accumulated over the years. Then, I got into the worst argument I ever had with my oldest son—one that brought me more pain and embarrassment. I had to look harder at myself, how I was impacting my kids, how I had hurt women I had loved. When we experience deep, painful moments in life, using artificial means to cope or just ignoring them does not solve our problems—does not help us learn the lessons of the experience.

For me, jumping from woman to woman and drinking was not the right way to deal with the painful relationships—because I love a life that is real and feels honest to me, and yet it was not me. Going from seeing your children every day to seeing them with less frequency and knowing your influence as a father in their lives has diminished drastically is something that brings deep pain to any caring father. So, I was in a rollercoaster of pain, and not taking the time to digest the lessons to be learned was clearly a big mistake on my part. I hope you, the reader, see that you can heal by facing the truth and asking for help, and by doing the deep work of assessing the lessons from the "failure." Remember that asking for help and support is the act of a brave person.

However, in spite of my pitfalls I am very proud of the man I have become and how I carry myself in this world. Today I am calm, centered, peaceful, and live life on my own terms—more than ever. That, my friends, feels amazing! Yes, I have a lot to learn, and I am getting there, but you can do better than me. Do not jump from one relationship to the next without learning the life lessons from them. You can be a better person for you and others by doing the internal work that relationships can teach us.

During any successful career there are often many failures. Actually, let's only call them "failures" if the person fails to learn from those experiences. I've struck out in life a few times, and I also won a few times! Even as a student I failed so many times that if you were to tell my former undergraduate or graduate classmates about what I have achieved, they would not believe that the person I am today is the same person they knew back then. Mostly because I learned to believe in myself and my confidence that everything will be fine is stronger today than yesterday. As a young person, we worry a lot and sometimes too much about what others think if we walk away from a relationship or job we hate—that is amazing, it shows strength. But it is that courage of doing the uncomfortable, what seems difficult, that offers the greatest opportunity to become a better version of yourself.

As I mentioned in the previous chapter, I wanted to become a mechanical engineer when I went to college. However, my grades and test scores (equivalent to the SAT) were not high enough to be admitted to the mechanical engineering department at the University of Puerto Rico–Mayaguez (this was and is today the best engineering school in Puerto Rico). Unwilling to give up on my dream, I figured out that another way would be to start as a math major at the University of Puerto Rico–Mayaguez, get good grades, and transfer into the mechanical engineering department. Well, I started taking courses in math, physics, and chemistry. I studied really hard but failed many times on my exams—I don't learn the way most people do and it affects how I take exams and even how I work with others. Yes, in my professional life, nobody knew this. Even when I think, to then write on paper is very hard for me; sometimes I create these big, amazing ideas and even formulate complex equations, but to then rewrite them in words in proposals or papers is a very challenging task for me. And it was my dear friend Laura Williams (yes, she is one of the editors of this book) who pointed that out to me and helped me big time. Friends, I wrote this book by hand in about four weeks, but to edit the book and polish sentences in a way everyone will follow took me almost two years. I learned late in life; I have a privileged mind but converting complex ideas or concepts to smooth persuasive language that everyone understands is extremely difficult for me.

Exams were challenging for me, but I later realized while in graduate school that doing the research, asking questions with a mentor, then designing an experiment or simulation to address them was my strength—and yes, it was so much fun for me. For the first time I felt I was smart, and I would love to be in an environment where I can do that, but I also love helping others while making a big difference in science. I also learned I cannot work in a setting where I am told what to do, how to solve a problem, and where someone else controls me. This is why I went to academia; I could have intellectual freedom, control of my time, and then decide what problems I want to research. When I learned from my PhD advisor what a professor does, I was hooked and committed to become one. But how to do it was my biggest dilemma, and we will talk later about this.

Friends, I learned that by having time to think and by engaging with the data or equation, not by taking exams, I learned more and can even come up with new solutions—that changed my life big time. And I hope you know that if you do not do well in exams, it does not mean you are not smart—your intelligence is hiding in some other way. I advise you to find an environment where you are given the opportunity to explore. This is why I encourage students to participate in summer research experiences to explore and test ideas in a supportive environment. There are many programs in the United States including the NASA Community College Aerospace Scholars (NCAS) and the Summer Undergraduate Research Fellowship (SURF) program at Purdue.

The sad part is that I learned in my 40s that I am very unique at building big bold visions and that I have unique brilliance in specific areas, but I need to be alone and quiet to think and then engage with others for that to happen, and yes, I need to be free to think without constraints and being micro-managed. Students today are faced with this problem and many sadly never realize their full potential because our rigid school system failed us—think of the anxiety and panic attacks that so many students suffer because they learn differently than the masses. Some students learn completely differently than our factory-type approach can teach, and the system that is forcing us to obey and not explore different ways of doing things fails to uncover and support the brilliance in these students. Perhaps you are one of these. Because of this, I teach courses where students work in teams, where they work on problems they choose and then they seek solutions based on feedback from their team members, myself as a coach in the classroom or in our research lab. Friends, use the suffering and hardship you experience to make the lives of others better.

When something caught my interest, I always wanted to dive deeper, to learn as much as I could about a topic. Unfortunately, that meant I didn't always study to pass exams. But I saw "friends" with very high GPAs buy or steal the exams; they cheated, big time. My grades seemed like those of a "failure." During that painful time in my undergraduate education, my friends and I were building our persistence and dedication muscles. These strengths were crucial to my success in graduate school and later as a professor! While those that took the easy road also graduated with engineering degrees and yes, better grades than me, years later I am the only one who is a superstar and reached the highest level of academia as a professor at a top university. Yes, many succeeded in industry or as businesspeople, but I could never trust anyone who cheated in college to be a trustworthy person—why? Because they will do it professionally too. Friends, integrity is important to me, and I hope you learn that becoming excellent is important, but who you become in the process is critical. Do you see yourself as a person who will be honest, even when it is painful? Is your integrity important to you? This is one of the reasons why

I am proud of the man I became; despite my failures in relationships, to be a man of integrity and excellence is super important to me. And people know that in my research or any faculty search, I will do the right thing—every single time.

Twenty years later I would not change my life for my peers that I saw cheating and taking the easy road. In the short term, what I was doing was not working, but I developed an insane determination and discipline skills. But failures in each stage in life could be the foundations for your big-time successful future life. Because of those "failures" I gained important life skills by learning to pick myself back up, persist in the face of discouragement, pursue the things that mattered most to me; and yes, I became a super-optimistic person in the face of challenges. For me, persistence has been a big catalyst for success; I will not accept a "No" from anyone. These skills paid off later; I'm in a position to be able to really work to make a difference in other people's lives. That satisfaction brings me so much joy and happiness that nobody can take from me.

Going back to my college years at UPR–Mayaguez, two and a half years later I devised another plan (Plan C): to transfer to the other engineering school Polytechnic University of Puerto Rico, even though mechanical engineering was not offered there. I decided to transfer since they were going to open the mechanical engineering (ME) degree in the next few years. After a year there, I decided I was not going to wait for a new degree to be created there, so I launched another plan—yes, Plan D. It was to apply to universities in New York—so I applied and got accepted to the State University of New York at Buffalo where they have a strong ME degree program, and the university was relatively affordable by US standards. I packed up my stuff and moved my skinny self to Buffalo, New York. This was a life-changing experience in many ways—blessings were rushing my way big time. In spite of the uncertainties, including financial resources, I had faith in myself and somehow I felt I had nothing to lose; plus, my parents cheered for me.

Despite the odds, I succeeded! In two years, I completed my BS in mechanical engineering. Seven years after that, I earned a PhD in mechanical engineering. A PhD in any field is achieved by only 2 percent of our US population. Less than 20 percent of that 2 percent become tenured professors in the United States, and only a small fraction of the small percentage gets permanent positions—yes only 0.4 percent become tenured professors, and only a small fraction of professors ever become endowed professors. Not only did I reach that level, but I did it at one of the top six engineering universities in the country! Now, imagine if you are a person of color—what will be your chances you will make it? Friends, if someone with a realistic mind knew this, they would say—Luciano, do not even bother to do a PhD, you will never become a professor and worse, you will never become a tenured professor or worse, an endowed chair professor. You need to listen to your inner voice—that quiet voice that talks to us; listen to it and have faith that what you are doing will eventually work out for you. There are no guarantees that even if you do all of this many of your goals will be achieved, but one more time, who you become is a gift you gained from that journey. I hate these words: "You need to be realistic." F— that and f— them. Until today, when someone tells me to be realistic, inside of me I am cursing at that person; in other cases I walk away or ignore them completely. You need to learn to ignore those negative, realistic mother—, period! Otherwise, you will live an average or mediocre life like many people in this world. Seriously! Please, friends, believe in yourself and have deep faith that the universe or God or whatever you believe is supporting you. I am cheering for you, and I want to hear your story one day. Your story will inspire others to climb higher!

It is possible to achieve something that less than 1 percent of the population can achieve if they have a big-time burning desire and are willing not to see failures as more than learning experiences, if they see them as successes in action. The man I became to be an endowed chair professor means more to me than the awards I received along the way—yes, I like them, do not get me wrong, and I am appreciative of them. When you achieve something so unique as that, you will change big time, and the man or woman you become is the true value in the journey toward your Epic Life. This is why I believe I am qualified to write this book, and why I have a lot to offer you as you climb the mountain of your Epic Life.

Today, I love how I live my life. I have control over my time and the way I carry myself. At 59 years old, I am in better physical, mental, and spiritual health than when I was 30. The confidence I have today and trust in myself and God is way to the roof compared to my younger self. I love myself more today than in my younger years. I only wish I could have told a younger me how it would all pay off—but that's why I'm telling you. If you are reading this book, I believe in you. Just keep pushing forward—you are a winner and you got this!

Let me share with you what happened along the way of getting my PhD. After I finished my BS, about two years later, I married for the first time—a woman that I felt a lot of love for. While the marriage was pretty much over after only a year and a half, I tried to avoid a divorce. About three years plus into it, we agreed it wasn't working, that divorce was the best solution. However, it broke my heart to know that I wouldn't be able to see my son much since they moved to another state. As tough as the breakup was, I grew tremendously from the experience. From that first marriage, I learned I love children and that I am insanely persistent in that which scares the average individual—I mean in spite of the fact the marriage was not working I never gave up on my goals and being part of my son's life. I will never give up my goals for anyone.

For now, the focus is the importance of learning from failures and that they are treasures in disguise—*failures are important lessons, gifts on the way to success.* The worst times of our lives often provide the potential for the most growth! They are gifts—diamonds in your backyard. From these examples in my own life, I hope that you are convinced that negative experiences and failures are only failures if you do not learn from them. As an evolving person with a growth mindset, you must be in a mode to learn every day—to grow a bit more—to study and synthesize new knowledge for you to apply now.

I always write down my goals—quarterly, monthly, weekly, and daily—in a notebook. Yes, daily goals. In the notebook, I evaluate experiences from the day, think about solutions to problems, and develop new ideas. In chapter 7, I will share with you how I start my day, how I use my morning to think, to study, to exercise, to put myself in a mental state to succeed, how I set my mind to know I will succeed today and get my body ready to deliver the best performance that day.

In learning from our experiences, especially those that are hard, one must understand the value of solitude. Quiet time for reflection provides us the time needed to digest lessons learned, to express gratitude to the universe or to God, or to plan the day to study and learn—a life of reflection is critical in our journey toward an Epic Life. Socrates said one must examine one's life. Similarly, a journal is a necessary tool to allow us to reflect. Reflection is part of our planning; then you must take massive action, collect data again, and then ask yourself: What is working? What is not working? Where do we make changes? From these insights you adjust and then take focused action, and yes, there will be times when you will have to make tough decisions—decisions that will conflict with your heart, but you will have to be brave and just do it! Remember how much I failed on my way to get my BS and PhD?

CHAPTER SUMMARY

As discussed throughout this chapter, keep in mind that you never need to be afraid of failure. If you approach life eager to explore, adapt, and change, you can be bold and pursue your deepest desires. Being willing to grow today supports your dream to build an Epic Life as you define it. Growth is not determined by achieving all your goals; the journey itself can help you become a better person, improving each day. Above all, please have faith in yourself and faith that you are protected by higher forces in the universe or God.

I'd rather regret the risks that didn't work out than the chances I didn't take at all.
— SIMONE BILES

CHAPTER ACTIVITY

ACTIVITY #4. Reflection Experiences

Time needed: Approximately 30 minutes.

4a. What can you learn from a recent failure or bad experience in your life?

4b. Can you recall a moment in your life when you persevered? Describe how you did it. What do you learn from it? Why is that experience unique for you? Can you recall another tough moment you pushed through?

4c. Write some ideas for solving a problem or, better yet, an "opportunity" you are facing.

4d. If you were a public company listed on the stock market or a national brand, which company shown in figure 1 would you wish to be: (a) top graph; (b) middle graph; or (c) bottom graph? Why?

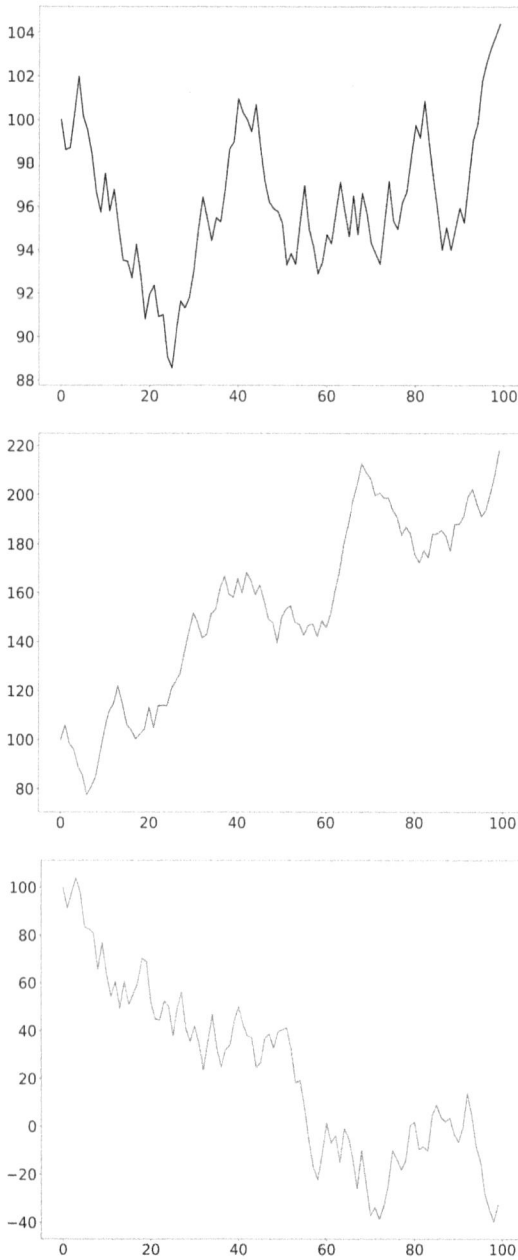

Figure 1. (a) Top graph: average around 95.5; (b) middle graph: positive slope; and (c) bottom graph: negative slope. Figures prepared by Dr. Venkatesh Pulletikurthi.

RECOMMENDATIONS

Books

The Obstacle is the Way. Ryan Holiday. Portfolio, 2014. A practical guide based on Stoicism that reveals how obstacles are not barriers, but hidden paths toward growth and personal excellence.

Daring Greatly. Brené Brown. Avery, 2012. A call to embrace vulnerability as the key to courage, creativity, and authentic connection. Failure becomes fertile ground for growth.

Black Box Thinking. Matthew Syed. John Murray, 2015. Compares how different industries handle mistakes, showing how accepting and learning from failures leads to better processes, decisions, and outcomes.

Biographies

Edison. Edmund Morris. Random House, 2019. A deep portrait of Thomas Edison, who failed thousands of times before inventing the electric lightbulb. His story illustrates how perseverance and curiosity conquer defeat.

Very Good Lives. J. K. Rowling. Little, Brown and Company, 2015. The author of Harry Potter shares how personal failures pushed her to discover her deepest calling. An invitation to redefine failure as a catalyst for purpose.

The Life You Want. Oprah Winfrey. Flatiron Books, 2023. The powerful story of Oprah, who turned a childhood marked by poverty and trauma into an iconic career of leadership, compassion, and global vision.

Movies

The Founder. Dir. John Lee Hancock. The Weinstein Company, 2016. Chronicles Ray Kroc's rise and the expansion of McDonald's—revealing both the achievements and ethical failures behind ambition.

Joy. Dir. David O. Russell. 20th Century Fox, 2015. Inspired by the real story of an inventor who overcomes rejection, betrayal, and financial hardship to build a business empire through unbreakable determination.

A Beautiful Mind. Dir. Ron Howard. Universal Pictures, 2001. Tells the story of mathematician John Nash, who, despite battling schizophrenia, makes revolutionary contributions to game theory and shows that mental struggle does not define one's future.

Works of Art

The Shipwreck, by J. M. W. Turner, ca. 1805. Tate Britain, London. A dramatic painting that captures human fragility against the forces of nature. Symbolizes how chaos can give rise to new forms of strength.

The Ruins of the Colossus, by Francisco de Goya, ca. 1810. Prado Museum, Madrid. Represents the fall of a once-invincible power. A visual metaphor of failure as a necessary stage for rebuilding with greater wisdom.

Phoenix: Symbol of Rebirth and Wisdom, by Tetiana Nyshchun (Italy). A vibrant depiction of the mythical Phoenix emerging from flames, capturing the essence of resilience and renewal.

4

On Mentors

Learning from Others' Journeys

We like to say that we don't get to choose our parents,
that they were given by chance—yet we can truly
choose whose children we'd like to be.
—SENECA

Mentors are those in our life willing to take the time to advise and support us personally and professionally, to help us become the best version of ourselves. Before we continue, I want to make clear the difference between a mentor and a role model. While at times I may use the terms interchangeably, a mentor is like a coach in that they are engaged in our success. A role model is someone we look up to but who is not directly engaged in our growth. A peer can be a role model when we have the opportunity to witness how they were able to succeed, but they may not work directly toward supporting our success. However, if a colleague works with you and helps you build a strategy for your career, or if they guide you, work with you, and teach you how they do things, then this individual is a mentor. In fact, in my career as a professor I worked with many superstar professors from whom I learned a lot. I learned how to be a better writer, a better scientist, and a better advisor by being shown both what to do and what not to do. Some of them had different political views than mine but I was focused on them as scientists, on what they had to offer in my field of study. That is what mattered to me at the time. I also interacted with leaders such as university presidents who were role models for me. I found their leadership abilities, their deep caring for others, and how they were as parents and spouses to be inspiring. One was the former president of Georgia Tech, President Bud Peterson, the most humble, caring, and successful individual I've been honored to encounter in academia. And at Purdue my former president, Mitch Daniels, is someone I considered a role model and someone who supported me a lot during one of my big projects, and I have great respect for his commitment toward making exceptional education available to everyone.

Later in this chapter, I will tell you about some of the mentors I had throughout my career, because at each level many people helped me get to where I am today. As Arnold Schwarzenegger likes to say, "You can call me anything you want but don't ever call me a self-made man." He believes, as do I, that nobody is truly self-made, that everyone receives some help and support along the way. If you are lucky enough to have parents who in addition to providing love and a safe environment in which to grow up were also mentors, treasure that!

A schoolteacher who said to you, "You can do it! You've got this!"; a neighbor who offered advice; or just about anyone that helped guide or advise you could be considered a mentor. Sometimes a single, brief interaction can make an amazing difference in your life. Mentors are often, but are not required to be, people that have achieved what we want or something close to it. They are individuals that know the path to success because they have lived it. Their knowledge, some gained from lessons learned from their personal failures in addition to their successes, can help us go farther along our own path. In my opinion, the best mentors are those who really care about us and have also achieved what we aim to achieve.

The great Sir Isaac Newton, discoverer of the key physics formula $F = ma$ (force equals mass times acceleration), wrote,

> *If I have seen further, it is by standing on the shoulders of giants.*
> —SIR ISAAC NEWTON

Mentors can play a key role in your success at any age. Have you ever seen a professional boxer, golfer, tennis player, or musician without a coach or several mentors? Of course not! Do you think that people playing sports or in music, art, or science do not have mentors? Look at the greatest quarterbacks, the Mike Tysons, Michael Jordans, Serena Williamses, and Lewis Hamiltons of the world; all had several mentors/coaches. None of us should be so arrogant as to imagine that we can achieve greatness without the guidance and support of others. So, when it comes to following your passions, be humble and learn from others who got there first!

In sports and music, mentors and coaches are expected to be part of the pupil's tools for success. Why would any individual seeking greatness not have one? Some people in science with whom I've crossed paths, as well as others I've come across in daily life, are incredibly arrogant. Some like to give the impression that they are so brilliant, they do not need any help from anyone. A world-class professor has a team of brilliant graduate students working under them so their great ideas can be executed. We all need support from others. The more one's team grows, the more successful they, as the leader, can become. The great motivational speaker Jim Rohn talks about surrounding yourself with the best people. He says that one becomes a product of the five people they hang out with the most. Building a positive group that is also going places is critical for your success. I tell my daughters and son, do not hang out with turkeys or chickens; surround yourself with eagles. Then, I tell them and my students the story of the baby eagle. There was a baby eagle that fell from the nest; then he was raised by chickens.

Throughout his life, he kept looking at the sky—the majestic eagles flying high and fast; he told his chicken friends, "One day I will fly like the eagles." They laughed and told him, "You can't fly, you are a chicken." The baby eagle was raised as a chicken but his potential as an eagle was there. One day he started flapping his wings and he took off and flew as high and fast as the eagles.

A mentor may be someone that impacts your life over a short or a long period of time. There comes a time when it feels right to let go of certain relationships—that is completely fine! It is not necessary to have the same mentor stick with you for five to ten years or more. However, some may be with you for a lifetime.

I am still in touch with my doctoral advisor, Dr. William K. George. He is like family to me. He helped me realize my dream of becoming a doctor of engineering. I love and respect him as a person and as a father. As we grow, mentors and role models help us mature and push us to perform at our best level. I was helped in this way by Dr. George, Prof. Richard Tapia, and by my dear friend Prof. Mark Glauser, a man that taught me how to write complex proposals and how to bring superstars together to play on my team. This is very difficult because in any field, for others to follow you, especially megastars, you must be perceived as one of them. If you can do that, you can achieve an even higher level of success than you probably ever imagined. As a person, you need to have amazing mentors, role models, and your tribe (like a lion's pride) to support you when times are tough—and you will support them when they need you. Lions can kill animals twice their size because they hunt as a team. In fact, there are other animals who are much bigger, but there is only one king of the jungle—the lion.

YOUR TRIBE

Find the best people to be part of your team, ones that you will help and support and that will do the same for you. Keep in mind that to get to that point you first must be the pupil and learn from the best you can find—how they do things, how they go about solving complex problems, how they think or create, and how they stay centered and strong. If you model your behavior on examples in nature, such as joining and later leading a "tribe," you will learn first to build a network of mentors and role models, and you will be off to a good start because you have the ingredients to achieve a lot. Let me share a true story.

What I am sharing is very personal and very emotional even as I write it. It goes back to a time that was extremely challenging for me in many ways. I am including it in the book because it was also a time during which I learned many important lessons, expanded the boundaries of my inner strength, and discovered new purposes for my life.

My oldest daughter was born at 31 weeks, nine weeks short of full term, with a serious lung disease and an open skull (*cutis aplasia*). She was a twin in utero. We, meaning her, my wife, and me, after saying goodbye to the twin that didn't make it, spent almost four months in the Neonatal Intensive Care Unit (NICU) at a hospital in New York City.

At the time I was an associate professor at Rensselaer Polytechnic Institute (RPI). I dropped everything to be with my then wife and our premature baby. There, my now ex-wife and I experienced day-by-day intense worry and pain, doing anything we could to keep our young baby alive. We fought for her life together with doctors, nurses, residents, and even the cleaning staff for the unit. I truly felt that everyone working in the NICU in any capacity was working and praying with us for our dear, our fragile baby to grow stronger, to be able to breathe on her own, and one day go home with her parents.

We were there together every single day for almost 22 hours daily. We formed friendships with other parents in a similar situation. We cried together when one of the babies passed. Her mom and I formed an alliance with her doctors and nurses, the ones at the hospital and the specialists on her care team. As a scientist, the best way I could help was to study her conditions, find the latest research, and reach out to the leading practitioners and researchers. I called doctors at Johns Hopkins and other top hospitals because I wanted to do anything I could to help our baby live. We fought for her every single day. I prayed intensely. I cried many times.

Fortunately, I was able to take a medical leave with full salary, taking the financial pressure off us. This is how I became close friends with **Mr. Curtis Powell,** the former VP of HR at RPI, who became a dear member of my tribe. He saw my pain and that of my former wife, and he did everything he could to give our baby a better chance at surviving by making sure I could be there with her and to advocate for her until she was released from the hospital. In addition to being a good friend, he has been a valued mentor and friend to me for over 20 years!

Therefore, in this chapter, I emphasize that a key component to becoming a world-class person in any field is in part dependent upon having others, especially great mentors and role models—yes, a community. This is why I love to study biographies—many heroes of our past are great role models for me.

ROLE MODELS AND MENTORS THAT CHANGED MY LIFE

My father, **Luciano Castillo Reyes**, was my mentor and a role model from early on. My dad worked hard in the Dominican Republic as a policeman. He later moved to Puerto Rico to become an appliance salesperson, at the same time studying and achieving his realtor's license. After building a successful real estate business, he created a unique car business in the late 1970s to the 1980s that installed custom audio systems, fancy wheels, and tires. And it was while working part time in his business that I learned the value of a strong work ethic and the value of being good at sales. My brothers and I learned many lessons working in our father's shop while growing up. Later in life, I realized how many of those lessons I use in my career as a professor. I saw him making a lot of money while remaining humble and being charitable. He had a burning desire to be more, to provide his family with a better life. My father was a leader, a champion in business and life, and in my view provided the foundation for all his children to be successful as individuals.

Let me clarify what I mean by success. I believe that a person that does their best achieves success. It is not tied directly to their bank account or prestige, but it is directly connected to a person becoming a full individual in every way. It is about being true to their values, their self-discipline, the way they carry themself, their overall view on life, and how they share their gifts with the world.

Being a Latin man, my dad was a strong father. Showing weakness was unacceptable. Although some fathers may be pushovers (truer nowadays; I have been there myself as a father), this was not my dad. In his house, if I screwed up, I would know it, and I was expected to earn my way back to the top. As the oldest son I was there to learn and help with his business. For me there was an expectation (it was a quiet expectation) that I would be there to lead and get the job done. He spoke to me with only a few words of advice, but those words were powerful enough to make a big impact on me today.

One day my dad and I were driving to visit one of his clients in the southern part of the island, in Peñuelas. As we drove, he pointed to a refinery and said to me, "Kilo [his nickname for me], do you see that? It was designed and built by chemical engineers—engineers solve problems." His comment sparked in me a deep curiosity about those engineers. I wanted to solve problems. From that moment on, my goal was to become an engineer—a mechanical engineer.

Looking back later in life, I realized the power of that moment and how my father planted the seed of my passion for solving grand social challenges with those words. Even though I disagreed with my father about almost everything, I respected him and the way he carried himself. He was a dignified man. My father was also extremely handsome and a visionary with the stature of greatness. I called him the Denzel Washington of the Caribbean.

Study the lives of great people and respect the opportunity you have today of being the best you can be regardless of your color or background. In a broader sense, mentors could be historical figures who did extraordinary things. Here are some of my mentors and heroes/ heroines: **Frederick Douglass** was a former slave who became the most photographed person of his time and advised Abraham Lincoln so Black men fighting for freedom in the Civil War would receive the same pay as white men. He was one of our abolitionists and a man I admire deeply. Although a slave, he learned to read, freed himself, then fought for other Black people to be free all the way to the White House and Europe.

Then my other idol, **Michael Faraday**, was the best chemist of his time. He grew up poor in England with no access to formal education. Faraday sought out knowledge and became a mentee of the best chemist of his time, Humphrey Davy. Michael Faraday grew to become a better chemist than Davy. He changed the way we look at electricity, magnetism, and experimentation. Both men changed my life. Sometimes, I think how Frederick Douglass would handle my situation and other times, I think of Faraday as a renewable energy scientist, and I try to conduct myself by imagining what he would have done in a similar situation. These are role models I have high respect for. **Muhammad Ali** is another big hero of mine, as is **Madame Marie Curie**, an amazing scientist who twice won the Nobel Prize, despite men not wanting to recognize her achievement, even helping wounded soldiers during World War I.

My academic father, **Professor William K. George**: I did my doctoral degree at the State University of New York in Buffalo under the supervision of Prof. George, a world-renowned expert in turbulence. When you are in an airplane and the pilot says, "Put on your seatbelt, we are experiencing a high level of turbulence for the next 30 minutes," you are feeling random motion, a consequence of random/chaotic motion in the sky. My research was on turbulence and an area of aerodynamics called boundary layers.

He not only shaped my thinking and approach to science, but he also gave me the courage to be bold, to be controversial, and to be myself. From him I learned the importance of figuring out who I truly am as a man, to be an independent thinker, to not simply follow the masses, and to always be honest as a scientist even when the truth is painful. He is an adventurous individual and truly a scholar in every way. In academia, we call the advisor under whom we do our graduate research our academic father or mother. They can drastically change people's lives. Prof. George changed my life—big time. I feel that it is my obligation to do the same for others. During the time that I was homeless, he shared food with me almost every day. During Christmas time he let me stay in his house while his family traveled. He brought me to spend time with his father and mother. His father, a devoted Christian pastor, would slip $50 in my pocket. He would pray for me and my family. His father was a truly beautiful human!

Prof. Mark Glauser, professor emeritus at Syracuse University: During my tenure as a young assistant professor at Rensselaer Polytechnic Institute it was my friend Mark Glauser who showed me what it takes to be a professor. He taught me many lessons. His brilliance and wonderful way of working with others led to multiple awards and nominations. To this day, Mark remains a close friend, a man I love dearly, and I still consider him to be a mentor since he continues to touch my life in many ways. He is so close to me that he performed the wedding ceremony for me and my second wife. I also think of Mark as my academic brother because he was also a student of Prof. George. Prof. Glauser was in a class 10 years ahead of me, an earlier member of our Turbulence Research Lab (TRL) "pride," as our "father" Prof. George likes to refer to us. Mark guided me, serving as both a mentor and a role model from my doctoral degree to a coveted role in a named professorship at Purdue University. Do you now see why having mentors and being part of a "pride" is critical to your success? Never take that lightly. We need our tribe, our "pride," to support us, believe in us, and push us to be our best.

Prof. Alexander "Lex" Smits: As a superstar scientist at Princeton University, he was an influential person in my career. I consider him both a role model and a mentor. During my PhD days he was one of the most highly respected people in the world and a competitor to my advisor. Our views differed, but both camps respected each other. Later, when I was a professor, he was always very friendly to me and wrote letters for my promotions. However, his biggest contribution to my success took place while at a bar during a conference for the American Physical Society. We were all drinking and partying, talking and having fun. At the time I was a new tenured associate professor at RPI. Proudly, I asked him, "Lex, what do you think about my research?" Guess what his response was? It was far from what I was expecting! He said, in his Australian accent, "Luciano, you are wasting your talent on boundary layers!" At the moment, it wounded my ego. It hurt! I couldn't believe he said that to me! Because he was someone for whom I had great respect and admiration, his opinion of my research contributions was very critical to me. However, after the initial shock, for weeks and months I kept thinking about what he said to me until I finally said to myself, "I will change my research path, big time!" And that was a big pivotal moment in my career, one that shaped who I became today. From that moment forward I took big, drastic risks on my research. I moved to wind energy, then biomedical engineering, then mass migration, then climate change. Listening to his harsh and honest feedback truly changed my life for the better. I do not think he has any idea that the brief exchange we had that day changed the direction of my professional career and helped me eventually become the Kenninger Chair Professor in Renewable Energy at a top six engineering school in the United States. My life changed because I listened to his honest feedback and for that I will always be grateful to him. Because I moved to a different field and I was early on wind energy, I rode a wave that has taken me very far—and brought so much fulfillment in my life.

Professor Charles Meneveau of Johns Hopkins University: A superstar professor with whom I worked for about 12 years. One of the legends of turbulence. Half Hispanic, half French, he is a citizen of the world and a scientist beloved by many. With Charles I learned to write proposals with the subtle differences that led to our work being funded, and together we brought our knowledge of turbulence to wind energy research. I learned from him the importance of diplomacy and a quiet pursuit of excellence. It was with his guidance that I fully became known as a "renewable energy guy" as my research shifted from turbulence in boundary layers to turbulence in wind energy. The way he writes and treats others made a big impact on me, and I considered him a mentor and role model, and a friend.

Prof. Richard Tapia at Rice University: One of my biggest mentors and role models is the great university professor Richard Tapia. He is one of the most resilient and brilliant men I have ever met. He told me to "hang out with big dogs because one day you will bark like one. Plus, people will think you are a big dog even if you are not." In academia, when a conference is named in your honor you know you have reached the top in your field. When the president of the United States invites you to the White House, you are a different beast! Richard Tapia not only dedicated his career to research in mathematics and operational research; throughout his career he always found time to mentor people from underserved communities. In this arena, he serves as an important role model for me; I watched him carefully. From the time I began teaching in the late nineties I have mentored minority students in STEM. Dr. Tapia is one of our giants. As a husband, Richard devoted his life to helping his late wife who fought MS for many years. He is a giant in every single way, a professor and a caring man you seldom find these days.

Prof. Fazle Hussain, distinguished professor at Texas Tech University: Dr. Hussain is a legend in the field of turbulence and was my partying buddy when I was in Texas. Now, in his upper eighties he is still writing papers and doing research like when he was in his fifties—yes, he is a beast! Although we disagreed big time on how to treat students, his passion for learning and for doing exceptional work is contagious.

From him, I learned how to best sell myself, my projects, and programs to key decision makers, to never compromise on excellence, and to always question my problem formulations to ensure that my work is unique. Prof. Hussain is a true legend. I enjoyed our time together in research, as well as our travels to France, Denmark, and Puerto Rico. He also taught me how not to tread on others.

Dr. Gina Lee-Glauser, the former vice president for research at Syracuse University: She is a force of nature and has zero tolerance for stupidity. I learned from her the importance of focus and effective communication toward others. She is the wife of my dear friend Mark Glauser. As I engaged with him on big projects, it was her skills in the art of building and selecting people for a team that drove successful initiatives. From her I saw firsthand the importance of caring and giving and yet having the courage to cut people off when necessary. A team is successful if one is surrounded with high-quality people who care about the mission. And in my quest to help others from diverse groups, she helped me see that as my major purpose in my career as a professor. And yes, she helped me with nominations and made fun of me big time on my screwups. A true champion, high-quality person in every way.

Laura Jane Williams, who has worked in senior roles advancing science at the University of Michigan: This is a person that is part of my inner circle and a person I trust 100 percent. In fact, if you noticed she is one of the editors of this book, that alone should tell you how I think and trust her. I learned big time from her the importance of image and presence. It was from her that I further grew as a leader by refining my big audacious goals into partnerships for innovations and learned to carry myself as the visionary leader I am. From her I learned to further expand why renewable energy is critical to our future of water security. Anything I do in my career, I bring her; and I am lucky to have a person like her with wisdom, persuasion, and the unique ability to see long-term trends. I also learned from her that how I think is often very complex and even though my ideas are insanely good (most of the time), how to articulate them for everyone takes unique reshaping, and Laura is the unique connector and a person I love! We need to learn our limitations, and if we are lucky to find people who care for us and whom we care for big time, we will propel our lives to unique levels.

MENTORS DON'T HAVE TO LOOK LIKE US

You may notice that most of my mentors and role models are men and white, but that is because my generation of engineers is almost all men. A mentor does not have to be like us or even be of the same race. Most of my mentors and members of my tribe do not look like me, and there are many women that changed my life big time that I am not including here. A role model does not even need to know that you have chosen them as such. If you have access to that person, it may be possible for them to slip into a mentor role without knowing it. This is a great way to glean knowledge from someone without making what could feel like a big ask of them since the time needed with them may be minimal.

You may wish to have a mentor that looks like you, someone that understands your background, where you come from, or that knows firsthand what it means to be you. However, if you restrict possible mentors to specific criteria like this, you could miss some incredible opportunities for learning and growth. My mentor during my PhD studies was a white man from Mississippi, a person from a completely different cultural background and who had some different views on how to treat others, especially scientists with different views, or even what fights to select. Yet, he was the best professor and best mentor I could have asked for at that time.

A mentor can provide support and will shine a light on you. Sometimes, these people are very demanding, like my friend Fazle Hussain. From him I learned to formulate deep questions in research and to never compromise on excellence. In choosing a mentor, pick people who will stretch you, who will tell you when you screwed up. If you can, learn how to think like them, observe how they do things, and adopt some of their approaches to your own way. As a mentee you will absorb and download the knowledge of the mentor with the freedom to erase whatever you want, or to use that knowledge to reach a deeper understanding of how to achieve your goals.

Be humble enough to admit what you do not know. Be curious and courageous enough to seek out mentors, and as with everything, be persistent. I will tell you that outside their area of expertise mentors may possess views or attitudes that you disagree with; that is okay. Do your best to put the differences aside, learn as much as you can from them on the subject matter at hand, then move on.

In my career, mentoring means working on scientific papers and proposals, or in organizing major professional conferences or being part of a board. I work with students as if I were a coach: I find their strengths and weaknesses, then I build programs and research problems to help them become amazing scientists. My goal is for them to find their unique talent and hopefully, their calling.

As I mentioned before, in life you need different mentors for different stages and purposes. While role models are generally thought of as people, keep in mind that numerous potential role models for you have written books. If you admire someone for the work they have done or the way they give back to society, read their book or biography to learn more about how they managed to achieve what they did. Read, take notes, and apply that new knowledge to your life.

I try to read one or two books per month. If you are serious about growing and willing to do the hard work like an individual trying to earn an Olympic gold medal, over time you will grow so much that people may not recognize you!

In addition to reading, I recommend you save money and attend workshops for self-development. I do it regularly. I make sure I take notes and build a plan of action to ensure I make good use of my investment. I do this at least once a year. I also attend professional conferences.

Find out what kind of opportunities might be out there to bring you into contact with people who have succeeded where you want to succeed, and work to get yourself in the same room with them.

Nothing worth having will come easily—you need to take the initiative to go and pursue what is burning deep inside of you. You must learn in a variety of ways. Study or listen to books, watch relevant You-Tube and history channels, and seek out knowledge and people that will help you be the best version of yourself (see recommendations of the at end of each chapter). Consider the amount of knowledge and number of experiences that an older person has, and how your life could be different if you could learn and apply only one to three pieces of advice from them. To get this type of advice it is often on us to reach out to others and to welcome the knowledge they offer us, even if it is painful.

When I travel, or when I'm in a restaurant, I always smile at others. If I connect with someone, I ask them which are their three favorite books of all time are. This is a great way to learn and find exceptional books that may change your life. Sometimes I ask them which book or mentor changed their life. One book or one inspirational movie could give you something that changes your life forever!

Always be on the lookout for nuggets of knowledge. Even people younger than us can teach us a lot. My daughters and my son are my best teachers on how to be more patient, more understanding, and more loving. From them, I am learning to be a better man so that they choose people around them who will elevate their lives.

As Arnold Schwarzenegger stated in many interviews, he is not self-made. Call him anything else, but not self-made. He emphasizes the people that helped him get to where he is now and the hard work he put in. To be where we are, we have had many mentors and role models, including great teachers and the support of our parents or caretakers. Beyond the classroom, we have many other teachers in our lives. They are people that broke our hearts, betrayed us, consistently outperformed us, stole from us, fired us, or discriminated against us. When you think about hurts and betrayals with a fresh perspective and an open mind, you can see that they were opportunities for us to learn *important* lessons. Challenging experiences, sometimes thought of as failures, can be our best learning opportunities. Painful experiences, when viewed properly, can be catalysts that help us evolve to be beautiful, strong, brilliant human beings! In fact, when I started writing this book, I was propelled by the pain of a breakup with my last partner.

Since mentors and role models are so valuable in our lives, cherish them. I am not saying to become friends with that verbally abusive lover or narcissist or toxic person that was detrimental in our development; far from it. Remember that it is important to *honor your "failures"* so that you can become a better version of yourself—an amazing individual that is about to emerge like a butterfly from a chrysalis. When you do this, you will change the world that exists deep inside of you! Remember, painful moments are hidden treasures—honor them, find the lessons, then move on!

So, seek out mentors and role models to help you grow. Notice your real-world teachers; honor the experiences, whether good or bad. Keep growing and growing! Life is a journey of learning about the gift of life, and most importantly, to learn who you are.

CHAPTER SUMMARY

Mentors are key people who guide us, challenge us, and push us to become the best version of ourselves. Unlike a role model, a mentor is actively involved in your growth. While both can inspire you, the mentor walks alongside you, coaches you, and shows you how to move forward—even through their own mistakes and setbacks.

Throughout life, we go through stages where different mentors appear from parents and teachers to colleagues, leaders, or even historical figures like Frederick Douglass, Marie Curie, or Muhammad Ali.

What matters is not that they look like us, but that they have the wisdom and experience we need at that moment.

The chapter highlights how surrounding yourself with a powerful "tribe"—your community that to supports you and uplift you—this is essential for your long-term success. Just like lions hunt in groups, we also need a team to achieve greatness. It also emphasizes that pain, failures, and disappointments can be great teachers if we are willing to learn. A mentor can be a brilliant scientist, a compassionate nurse, or even someone who broke your heart.

Finally, the chapter invites us to actively seek mentors, read biographies, attend workshops, ask questions, and never stop learning. Because, as Arnold Schwarzenegger says, no one makes it alone. And you don't have to either. Life is a journey to discover your greatness—with the help of those who have walked the path before you.

CHAPTER ACTIVITIES

ACTIVITY #5. Role Models

Time needed: Approximately 10 minutes.

5a. Write the names of five people that you consider to be role models or mentors of yours. Why?

5b. What books, podcasts, or other media have you looked to for guidance?

RECOMMENDATIONS

Books

Tuesdays with Morrie. Mitch Albom. Doubleday, 1997. A student meets weekly with his dying professor, who shares life lessons on love, work, forgiveness, and meaning.

The Wisdom of Elders. Marc Freedman. PublicAffairs, 2008. Explores how intergenerational mentoring can enrich both mentor and learner, and be a key to building more humane societies.

Tribe of Mentors. Tim Ferriss. Houghton Mifflin Harcourt, 2017. A collection of interviews with extraordinary individuals who share tools and life lessons that have guided their paths.

Jonathan Livingston Seagull. Richard Bach. Scribner, 2014. The story of a seagull who dares to fly higher than the rest and, in doing so, becomes a teacher to others. A parable about overcoming and shared learning.

Mastery. Robert Greene. Viking, 2012. Explores how to achieve excellence through continuous learning and mentorship. Includes historical examples of people who mastered their art thanks to great guides.

The ONE Thing. Gary Keller & Jay Papasan. Bard Press, 2013. Teaches how to focus your energy on what truly matters to achieve extraordinary results. A book that acts as a practical mentor for your productivity.

Biographies

Socrates: A Life Examined. Luis E. Navia. Prometheus Books, 2007. Explores the life of the great Greek philosopher who taught through dialogue, becoming one of the most influential mentors in history.

I Know Why the Caged Bird Sings. Maya Angelou. Random House, 1969. A lyrical work that shows how the author transformed pain and discrimination into wisdom and leadership through the power of words.

Memories, Dreams, Reflections. Carl Jung. Vintage, 1961. Reflections from the father of analytical psychology, offering guidance for exploring the mind, the soul, and deep personal growth.

Movies

Dead Poets Society. Dir. Peter Weir. Touchstone Pictures, 1989. A passionate teacher inspires his students to think for themselves and live with purpose, igniting their desire to make a difference.

Good Will Hunting. Dir. Gus Van Sant. Miramax Films, 1997. A young man
with exceptional talent is guided by a mentor who challenges him emotionally and spiritually to recognize his own worth.

The Karate Kid. Dir. John G. Avildsen. Columbia Pictures, 1984. The wise
guidance of a martial arts master transforms an insecure teenager into a
strong, balanced, and disciplined person.

Works of Art

The School of Athens, by Raphael, 1509–1511. Vatican Museums, Vatican City.
A fresco celebrating knowledge and teaching, featuring the great mentors
of Western philosophy, such as Plato and Aristotle, at its center.

Saint Jerome in His Study, by Albrecht Dürer, 1514. Private collections and
museums. A work that portrays dedication to knowledge, contemplation, and the transmission of wisdom—representing the ideal of the wise
mentor.

5

Mastery

Becoming Exceptional!

> *Hard work outweighs talent—every time.*
> —KOBE BRYANT

My favorite book of all time is *Mastery* by Robert Greene. Greene brilliantly articulates how exceptional individuals achieve greatness with focused dedication over an extended period of time. But first, you need to know what you will commit to for your life's work! I was fortunate to have a good idea in my early twenties, as many people do. But others find a new passion later in life, and still others are lucky to discover multiple hobbies or areas they love to devote their time to. You may be surprised when I say that the method to mastery is the same, regardless of your purpose. It's vitally important to focus on your whole person, and I've divided this holistic approach into five focus areas of your life, but they are all connected and equally important: for example, (1) Family and Friends, (2) Health, both Physical and Mental, (3) Finances, (4) Self-Mastery or Service, (5) Career or Business. However, you can decide your priority areas according to your values. These five areas will be a good starting point for everyone. This is how you will pursue your Epic Life.

In this chapter, I want to encourage you to uncover that burning desire deep inside of you and to focus on that purpose or objective and give it your all, so that you achieve mastery in something (e.g., musician, engineer, scientist, community leader, sports, medical doctor, etc.). In what area or field do you want to be amazing so that you benefit society?

PURSUIT OF EXCELLENCE BY EXPOSURE

The objective now is for you to pursue excellence in a specific area such as sports, art, science, business, politics, or something else that you are drawn to. If you are in sales, for example, learn as much as you can about connecting with others, engaging with people, and closing a sale. In addition to your college courses and internships, get some books that will help you become a better business leader or begin a small business with some friends. Even though we are referring to a career, the pursuit of excellence can be tailored to any area of your life that you're passionate about; for example, becoming an exceptional parent and raising strong, independent children who will become well-adjusted individuals that uniquely contribute to the progress of our human race. What you focus on is up to you; this is very personal, and it is your choice of the area of your life that you wish to master.

For instance, a person may want to pursue mastery in the understanding of love. The books *The Five Love Languages: How to Express Heartfelt Commitment to Your Mate* and *The Five Love Languages of Teenagers* by Baptist pastor Gary Chapman outline five general ways that romantic partners, or parents and teens, express and experience love. Chapman calls these "love languages." While the focus of these books is on romance and parent–child relationships, the underlying theories translate well to other interpersonal relationships. His method of figuring out how to have successful relationships is about recognizing that one's own emotional needs and those of their partner or children can be translated to friendly and collegial relationships. How do you become a mature adult? Above all, learn about yourself, about who you are at this point in your life and what matters to you.

If you are a professional athlete, you can never settle for an average performance, but if your focus in life is becoming a world-class chef, then being average as an athlete is perfectly okay. However, as a chef you want to achieve mastery. You want to pursue excellence and be exposed to different cuisines, flavors, food specialties, and so on. Go and do a study abroad in Italy or Japan or go to Argentina or Vietnam. Give yourself the opportunity to learn from others and see how different flavors bring a unique expression of you as a chef. Find a way to ensure that when people eat your food, they experience something unique in the way you present the dish or the flavors. As a chef, push yourself to be the best you can regardless of what others are doing—here is where you bring your burning desire, your passion, your focused energy so that you express yourself in a unique way that is you. Something worth pursuing is rarely easy and takes many years of focused efforts. Achieving excellence takes time, takes trial and error; it means being an assistant to the chef, so you learn from others how it is done. Even when you begin cooking in a restaurant or if you simply want to be a great cook for your children or partner because this is how you express love for them, be patient with yourself. It may take several screwups, or you may have to practice and practice so that you can perfect your cooking skills. In life, it is important to learn that things take time, and how you express yourself in this world is unique to you. You do not need to be like your siblings or your friends; if you find your passion, that area in which you feel a deep burning desire to achieve mastery—this is a gift. But, if you do not know what that area is, my friend, expose yourself to different activities (e.g., experiences that are not detrimental such as drugs or alcohol, etc.); while in college learn about drama; get involved in a professional society in something you find interesting; play different sports; or if you can travel, take road trips to see nature or hike small mountains; or visit museums. By exposing yourself to different activities, one thing will click for you. Even something such as riding a bike or filming your friend roller skating could spark a unique interest in becoming a videographer or movie producer. Friends, I always wanted to write an inspirational book to help others, but do you know when I had the urge to do it? Yes, when I was experiencing deep pain.

Suppose as a child your learning disability caused you so many challenges adjusting in school or even getting good grades, but that pain then created the fuel for you to learn everything you can about learning disabilities, and then as you learned more and more over time, you became a teacher; then you started building your own unique courses that bring engagement and foster creativity in your students. You became a favorite teacher and one day you said: I am going to create my own school. And that school changes how we nurture students in ways that the traditional manufacturing style of teaching cannot do. Sometimes the greatest gift lies in our painful experiences. Seeing a need to help others because of your own detrimental experiences can be the fuel you need to achieve mastery in each area that matters to you. And this passion of yours in that area will make a difference in the lives of other children that are victims of an educational system not tailored to support their learning style. You can help others blossom and in the process you become an agent of hope and change for our society. Does that make sense?

Pursue a life that matters to you, find something in which you would like to achieve mastery—something that brings you passion and joy, in which you can immerse yourself for hours. In that little bubble there is a gift for you—when you dedicate hours and hours and you learn lessons, you can polish some skills and then your job is to find how you share your special gift with the world.

Imagine that you love painting, and visiting museums and learning different styles is something you can do for days; but you have learned that when you paint you calm your mind, you become less anxious, and you even feel deep happiness and joy. And because of this unique passion you feel, one day you make the decision to study psychology in college but decide to build your program in a way that integrates art: specifically painting in your degree of psychology. Because of your own challenges with anxiety and your superactive mind, you find a unique way to help others; your own challenge becomes a gift to help others. You learn about styles and even how different artists (e.g., van Gogh) have struggled with mental illness, so that you bring all of that in the way you help your clients. And as you learn and learn, and you perfect your style, you become a unique therapist who can help people. This, my friend, is what I am talking about in using your burning desire, your passion, and challenges to achieve mastery in a specific area so that your own pain becomes a blessing to others.

Young friends, you do not need to be like everyone else; your struggles and challenges in early life could be the seeds for you to be a blessing of hope to others. However, it is difficult to deliver a world-class performance in all areas of life, and you need to learn that you have other areas that you need to manage such as your finances, your health, your family and friends, and your career. Find a way to do something each day in some of those areas. We will talk more about those in later chapters. For now, I want you to have a sense of your passion, what brings you joy; then devote years in that area to achieve mastery—to pursue excellence to your own standards. Start deciding early; the most important opinion or person you need to satisfy is yourself.

If you are actually lucky enough to find your gift early, then move in that direction. Thus, later you will see how we select those areas that matter most to you and then focus on a given field of expertise. For example, I am not suggesting you can become a world-class attorney but disregard your health or your family. The goal is to identify four or five key areas (e.g., Health, Family and Friends, Finances, Career, Mastery) that are important in your life and put effort into them on a regular basis. Some weeks you will dedicate more time to one area than others.

This is about managing your life while you pursue excellence in each field—pursue mastery, but you must take good care of your health (e.g., mental, physical, and spiritual) everyday!

For example, every day I send a positive text to each of my children to encourage them, to tell them "I love you." Sometimes I send my daughters a short video that has a lesson I want them to learn. These are ways I help ensure our family machine remains solid. Other times, we have dinner as a family. When we do little things, they can make a big difference over time (check out the book *The Compound Effect* by Hardy). It is very important to learn how to identify things that can make a big difference. Another book on the topic is *The One Thing* by Gary Keller et al. (2013).

Moreover, a healthy body is important because to perform at a high level or to achieve mastery one needs to be in the best condition possible. I simply avoid sugars, soda, fried food, and heavily processed food; no alcohol, no drugs, and so on; I try to get six to seven hours of sleep per day (though I rarely hit my target, often getting less than six); I go to all of my routine medical appointments; and I train and compete in triathlons to keep myself motivated to exercise regularly. This helps me keep my physical body in good shape (excellent for a regular person but not at the level of a top athlete).

I think of health as all encompassing—physical, mental, and spiritual. Because of that, I do things every day to support myself in each of these areas. I've talked about the physical a bit. Let's move on to brain health since it is very important. We must "work that muscle" to keep it healthy. Later we will talk in depth about all these areas. Even though my aim is not to become a world-class athlete, I train every day to have a mind that is relaxed, centered, and peaceful; and for that I have specific activities (e.g., daily journal, meditation, daily gratitude, and sauna time, and a few times a week I get into an ice bath). A healthy body, mind, and spiritual balance is critical to experience life to the fullest and to experience moments of joy.

In my career as a professor and scientist, I have focused on delivering a world-class performance every day for over three decades. As a father,

I tried to be world class, and as for my finances, I make sure they are very solid, staying debt free and have strong emergency funds in place. Knowing what is important to you will help you prioritize your time so you can best focus energy to achieve mastery in the areas of your desire.

As you dedicate many years of your life to achieving mastery—training for the Olympics, or you are in medical school to become a cardiologist, or in law school, or studying to become a nurse or a psychologist—you want to be able to keep the rest of your life in balance, so it is important to ensure you have your finances in order (do not spend more than your income, do not max out credit cards), stay healthy, have a strong family and friends support system, and so forth.

If you are a schoolteacher, be a teacher that inspires their students. Be one that touches the lives of your colleagues or your students or your community. I urge you to be the best teacher you can be; do not be a boring average teacher that is there to collect a paycheck; instead be the best you can because that is how we touch many lives. Go out of your way to be an inspiring/exciting teacher. If you are a mechanic, then be the best mechanic you can be. Do things because you believe in them and they are important to your mission in this life. And this is success; be your own person and define where you are going as an individual that is pursuing mastery—excellence.

You may wonder, "How can I become exceptional if I keep failing, like Luciano did in his younger years?" There is a way! The purpose of this book is to help you find the way—never give up! As part of the process, in the next section, we will discuss burning desire so that even when things are going the wrong way, even when all you see is no, you will never give up because of that fuel inside of you—the burning desire.

A BURNING DESIRE TO WIN

Napoleon Hill, in his landmark book *Think and Grow Rich,* states that a person must have a burning desire to achieve their dreams. Remember how many times I failed when I was in college? Because I had a big burning desire to achieve my goals, I kept working hard and trying different approaches until I reached my goal, in spite of the many failures I experienced.

Whatever you want to do, if you want to be great at it, you have to love it and be able to make sacrifices for it.
—MAYA ANGELOU

I knew I wanted to be an engineer but had no idea that I was going to become a superstar professor! No way, not in my dreams, but it happened because I never gave up. My disadvantages in learning style required me to work harder than the average engineering student. But this extra effort translated into work ethic and discipline, which paid off big time over my entire professional life. Your own struggles early in life could indeed become your major superpower later in life—do not underestimate your struggles. When I was able to move to an area like research where one gets to work on a single problem for many years, and I was able to use my creativity to find a solution that didn't exist, I shined big time! I was in my element, in my strength, and I killed it big time! But you will ask, how did I know I was in my element? Well, first I was so comfortable, and I was happy working on my research even when there were so many uncertainties like money and not knowing if I was going to graduate. I felt at home, and I was happy, and believe in me, I faced many big challenges including not speaking English, and the financial burning was real, and not having my family was very hard. But that burning desire to be more, to achieve my dreams was driving my efforts.

As we grow from teenagers into our twenties, thirties, forties, and so on, new interests and passions will emerge. At each stage of life, there are valuable lessons to be learned. Enjoy each stage without worrying about having everything figured out. As I approach 60 years of age, I think about the gifts I will leave behind so the lives of others can be better and the lessons I have learned that I can share with my children, my students, my grandson, and even people I meet when I travel.

I learned early on the value of earning one's way in life and the importance of finding, deep inside ourselves, our unique talents and gifts. Then, with these gifts, we must find a way to solve problems in society in order to help others. The more people you help and the more impact you make in the lives of others, the better your life becomes. Giving to or sharing your gift with others is a way to achieve an Epic Life and fulfillment in your own life. Over time, you will discover new gifts or different ways to share your gift with others.

Achieving mastery in one area could be combined in a unique way to make a big impact in other areas. For example, for more than 20 years I have been a professor, but writing this book and doing workshops about building your Epic Life is a way to expand *my purpose in life, which is to make the lives of others better by bringing hope, energy, and knowledge.* Everything I do in my life is centered around this vision for my life. Later in this book you will learn how to find your purpose in this life, and if you align your gift or gifts with it, you will have a life that is meaningful—an Epic Life!

It took me many years to learn what my purpose in life is and find my unique gifts; so please, my dear friends, be patient with yourself. Life is a journey of discovery, and as you get older and explore who you are, all these pieces come together. I tell my teenage kids, I am almost 60 years old, and I am still finding what I want to do with my life. So please relax; you do not need to know everything at 17 or 19 or even 30. Please, do not fall into the trap of thinking that everyone else's life is perfect because of what you see in social media. Make your life your masterpiece and build your own games and rules.

For example, this book is the culmination of years of work with my graduate students and teaching in ways that really make an impact on how we train students to solve problems that matter in society. My career as an engineering professor provided me with a vehicle to achieve a big part of my life's purpose and touch many lives while bringing knowledge and energy to others. I am, at my core, a humanitarian engineer—yes, I made that up because I never see myself as a mechanical or aerospace engineer or environmental engineer. My work is in solving problems to make our society better, to help improve the lives of my students and bring energy security to people around the world—we are making a big impact in this world, and this brings me deep satisfaction because I am in the pursuit of my life's purpose. Thus, achieving mastery in each area and aligning that with your gift toward a purpose in life is indeed a way to achieve an Epic Life.

For me as a person, life's purpose and my role as a professor is to see people doing well, which brings me a lot of joy. My happiest moment is when my students graduate and I look back at the long journey we took together. At that moment, I know that they are equipped with the skills needed to be the best they can be as researchers and as problem solvers.

My early experiences in sport and as a student taught me that to push and push to bring my burning desires into achieving my goals was valuable, but the person I was becoming every time I overcame huge obstacles was the best—the young man I was becoming was something I did not notice until later in life. As I write this book, I turned 59 just a few weeks ago, and I have the desire to share some tools to help you succeed and to know you must have hope and that there are many of us cheering for you.

BECOMING EXCEPTIONAL: INTENSE AMOUNT OF PRACTICE EVERY DAY FOR MANY YEARS

Consider the number of years and amount of time that a surgeon works to get to that level. Lewis Hamilton of Formula 1 racing spent hours and hours as a child training with his father. If you read the story of Kobe Bryant, you will learn that even when he made it to the NBA, even when he was considered a megastar, he was the first on the basketball court at every practice. He outperformed his colleagues, and even in the off-season the man not only trained for basketball but also worked hours each day to strengthen his body and to increase his vertical jump and his speed. The superstar had a coach working with him to help him become the great Kobe Bryant, as did Serena Williams, the best tennis player of all time, and the great Simone Biles who revolutionized gymnastics and is considered the greatest gymnast of all time. From dealing with mental health to becoming a world-class gymnast is indeed a remarkable achievement. What I am saying, my friend, is that you can write your goals, and you can pray each day, but until you get your butt on the court or to the medical school, your goals will remain dreams. Massive action will repeatedly beat talent if the talent does nothing but sit on the couch!

Now, when you learn to focus your energy, think like a laser light, focus your energy on a specific, narrow goal needed to achieve mastery—this type of intense focus is power! Think what we can do if we put intense energy on a material—we can cut metals or any solid material with precision using a laser. This narrow focus is what I want you to have in something—to focus everything you've got into one area—one thing (e.g., your business; to achieve a supreme level of health with a strong, lean body: swimming; your PhD, etc.), at least at the beginning. Even when you focus your energy you still need to bring in other resources such as the following: (a) have mentors and role models; (b) build your community of support or your tribe; (c) gain new knowledge and improve your communications skills; (d) change your peer group; (d) improve your diet and nutrition, which includes water; (e) improve your physical and mental conditioning routine. To achieve an audacious goal to build that Epic Life you dream of, you cannot be the same person you were last year—a new you must be born and allowed to grow.

It is important that once you know what you want and have a burning desire, that you remain focused! And know that you will need to spend many years of steady focus until you get there. Success is not like fast food; rather, compare it to a marathon, which requires many small steps to reach the finish line—one must build a solid foundation for strength and endurance, constant daily training over many months. As a first step, do not think about becoming outstanding from the get-go. The success achieved by the Simones of the world took many years of training and learning from failures and even overcoming setbacks, such as dealing with mental health challenges—overcoming them made her the best gymnast of all time. You need to be aware that the fast-food mentality does not lead toward an Epic Life in the long run! When Simone was training and training and training, she was building a solid foundation—both mentally and physically. This is why I want you to appreciate the importance of daily discipline, even if it is small steps, and the importance of having a strong foundation in five key areas: (1) Health: Body-Mind-Spirit; (2) Finances; (3) Family and Friends: your tribe, your community; (4) Career; and (5) Self-Mastery—these are the five pillars for an Epic Life!

THE LONG-TERM GAME

First, you must build a foundation of good habits that will make you excel in your chosen area, whether it be athletics, music, science, fashion, or culinary arts, among others. Think of a maestro in music. The individual may have started playing music just as a fun activity, perhaps encouraged by a caregiver, but over time learned to enjoy it at a level that it became a daily practice. Years passed and the person kept practicing. Then one day, they decided to become a professional piano player; then hired a new teacher, then studied music in college, and on and on. From a recreational activity as a child to a competitive career, it was a long journey to become a maestro.

For a professor to get tenure it takes many years; after undergraduate study, you go to graduate school (5 to 7 years), then a postdoc (two or three years). Then, if you are lucky enough to be offered a tenure-track position, you will be an assistant professor seeking tenure, which takes about six years (associate professor), then about another five years to go from associate to full professor. If you are lucky, you could become an endowed chair professor in five to ten years. Friends, it takes time to achieve mastery and a level of excellence that others recognize, if they ever do. Think of the long journey a neurosurgeon must endure to save lives.

To get there you need to keep nurturing your good habits by learning how to get better over time and learn from your setbacks. Which skills do you need to develop in your field? Who can help you? What resources will you need to get access to coaches, courses, workshops, training camps? For example, if you are a scientist, you will need to be a good communicator, including being an excellent speaker so that you can clearly convey complex problems in a way that everyone will understand. And guess what? You need to persuade funding agencies to support your research so that you can have graduate students in your lab. In fact, excellent communication skills can help you achieve more in life in any area including in business, arts, politics, and so on. So, in summary, it is critical that there is that strong burning desire inside of you to keep pursuing that one thing that you are passionate about.

Building expertise is necessary in anything you wish to pursue, and it is a lifelong quest. The initial chapter started with you being a winner already. As we move from various jobs and from a regular life to the building of an Epic Life, we must see this journey as one toward becoming great, even if we initially suck! But you decide what that means for you. Practice even if it is a bad performance, then practice more and more until you reach the level needed to reach your goal, keeping in mind that you may not see noticeable progress for years. However, continuous hard work for a long period of time will help you develop expertise (see the books at the end of the chapter).

CHAPTER SUMMARY

Mastery is a long journey that requires mental preparation and faith that you will achieve your goals. Life is uncertain, my dear friend, and it is important that you have faith in yourself and in something. You will never be 100 percent sure that this is the path that will work, but the faith in you about what you are doing will tell you it is okay! Even if you change your path, stay flexible and adjust.

Today we have electricity, something that we take for granted. Visit any developing country where electricity is not dependable, and you will appreciate the benefits of AC and the consistency of nice, warm showers. Think about all the engineers and entrepreneurs who worked on these problems for so many years to make our lives so convenient. For example, think of the great Nikola Tesla and of Michael Faraday, who rose from poverty to become an illustrious scientist who paved the foundations for the Tesla induction motor.

Eliminate a quick-fix mentality from your life! Keep making little efforts even if they are not good, but keep progressing bit by bit; one step forward each day. Then take one more step, work one more hour, study a bit harder, run one more mile, or read 10 more minutes. Always push a bit more to make that a habit for your life of going the extra mile. And if you do all of that but decide to change your bachelor's degree from engineering to biology or from being a mechanic to creating your own business or starting a new direction in your life—guess what? You have developed the discipline to start all over again.

Know that the old-fashioned way of continuous hard work will be needed. Of course, if you can get used to fast-track progress, use the advances in research to do a new exercise that makes you stronger or a new way of exposing your body to cold/hot temperatures to make you more mentally resilient. With a necessary coach, proper vitamins, and books, you are the only one who can do the work! A champion is made at the gym day after day, even when nobody's looking. Do the necessary work to be the best version of yourself even if nobody notices that. The painful moments that broke your heart—use them to propel you forward to become a better version of yourself. Have the discipline to save your money even if it is $5 dollars a week, so that later you can buy your car and dare to pursue a great life that one day you will be proud of. These small habits may be difficult, but later you will enjoy the smell and sound of your new machine!

Doing what is difficult paves the road to success, to building an epic day, an epic year, and then an Epic Life. When you see any bumps in the road as opportunities for learning and growth, they can help you stay aware of the direction you are headed in. Getting up at 5:00 a.m. to swim, run, or bike is difficult and cold at times, but later you earn the right to finish a triathlon even if you are not the first overall—like me, I just want to finish them and feel happy. I do a triathlon every year. Is finishing first place the best or even winning? Not at all. My friend, it is the person that you become! This is why pursuing big, audacious goals matters to me!

As you pursue a burning desire to become a better you, that translates into a better society because now a child, father, or mother has a son or daughter showing up! You inspire others to become better, and you become a better leader by doing so. You can improve society and, thus, the world! Therefore, encouraging others to become better is great for everyone, but it begins with you.

As you embark on a path of mastery toward greatness, you can see why having a burning desire to pursue what you deeply think about day in and day out is important and how having a coach or role models is critical for your success. You will also discover that on your journey toward achieving mastery, you will have many shortcomings, as I have. Your job and that of your team is to find those weaknesses and find ways to address them—but build on your natural talents—in that direction is your gift.

Think of a boxer like Floyd Mayweather, with nearly 60 wins and zero losses! Do you think he worried only about boxing in the ring? No, he worried about marketing his brand, how he sold himself to the media, how to promote his fights so that he was paid—and he always got paid! He also worried about finances and how to manage his money, his mental state, even his nutrition and having the best team around him. All aspects of his career required proper planning and coordination so that he could keep winning as he did—being exceptional in the ring! Boxing is a business to achieve mastery.

CHAPTER ACTIVITIES

ACTIVITY #6. Focus Area

Time needed: Approximately 25 minutes.

6a. In what area would you like to achieve exceptional performance? Why?

6b. Which areas are very important to you? Write down your top five areas. Here are my top five areas that I work on every day: (1) Health; (2) Finances; (3) Family and Friends; (4) Career; (5) Self-Mastery.

RECOMMENDATIONS

Books

Mindset: The New Psychology of Success. Carol Dweck. Ballantine Books, 2006. Explains how adopting a growth mindset—instead of a fixed one—can transform your life. It teaches us that our abilities can be developed through effort, the right strategies, and continuous learning.

Grit: The Power of Passion and Perseverance. Angela Duckworth. Scribner, 2016. A powerful reminder that success depends not only on talent but on the combination of passion and perseverance over time, even in the face of failure.

Awaken the Giant Within. Tony Robbins. Free Press, 1991. This personal transformation guide invites you to take control of your emotions, finances, body, and relationships to awaken your inner potential.

Jonathan Livingston Seagull. Richard Bach. Scribner, 2014. An inspiring fable about a seagull that refuses to live limited by what others expect of it. It's a call to follow our dreams and fly beyond self-imposed limits.

Mastery. Robert Greene. Viking, 2012. Explores how to achieve excellence through continuous learning, observation, and deliberate practice. Includes inspiring stories of geniuses like Leonardo da Vinci and Michael Faraday.

Think and Grow Rich. Napoleon Hill. Tarcher, revised edition, 2007. A classic on how focused thoughts and beliefs can create wealth. Based on interviews with the most successful entrepreneurs of the 20th century.

The Magic of Thinking Big. David J. Schwartz. Touchstone, 1987. Teaches how ambitious thoughts, self-belief, and decisive action can open doors to great achievements, both personal and professional.

Life Without Limits. Nick Vujicic. WaterBrook, 2012. The author, born without arms and legs, shares his inspiring story of faith, resilience, and purpose, proving that no barrier is insurmountable with self-love and determination.

Biographies

The Greatest: My Own Story. Muhammad Ali. Random House, 1975. The autobiography of Muhammad Ali, revealing his personal struggle inside and outside the ring.

My Life: Queen of the Court. Serena Williams. Simon & Schuster, 2009. An intimate account of the champion Serena Williams and the challenges she faced in her career.

Faster than Lightning: My Autobiography. Usain Bolt. HarperSport, 2013. From his humble childhood in Jamaica to becoming the fastest man in the world.

Movies

Rocky. Dir. John G. Avildsen. United Artists, 1976. The story of an unknown boxer who proves the value of perseverance.

Coach Carter. Dir. Thomas Carter. Paramount Pictures, 2005. A coach who demands academic excellence and character from his players.

Rudy. Dir. David Anspaugh. TriStar Pictures, 1993. A young man pursues his dream of playing football against all odds.

Works of Art

David (1501–1504), by Michelangelo. Galleria dell'Accademia, Florence. Represents bravery in the face of the impossible; a symbol of human courage.

Nike of Samothrace (ca. 190 BC), unknown artist. Louvre Museum, Paris. A classical sculpture that celebrates victory and triumphant effort.

Atlas Holding the Sky (classical mythology). Various historical representations. A mythological figure symbolizing the burden and responsibility of holding the world.

6

Becoming a Trailblazer

Do not go where the path may lead, go instead where there is no path and then leave a trail.
—RALPH WALDO EMERSON

Before the '80s, you hardly ever saw a Black person, or any person of color, play professional tennis. It was the legendary Arthur Ashe who won singles at Wimbledon, the Australian Open, and the US Open. Clearly these achievements as the first Black person in professional tennis make him a trailblazer.

Later, Serena Williams was a trailblazer too—not only because she retired as the greatest tennis player of all time, but because of her dedication to becoming an exceptional athlete and her grace during interviews. By her incredible achievements, she opened the door much wider for others, especially people of color, to join the tennis court. She had a mentor—her father—who demanded the best from her and her sister. With training and commitment and her burning desire, she eventually became *The* Serena Williams.

Lewis Hamilton, a seven-time Formula 1 world champion, is an amazing example of greatness. Anyone who achieved such a level of success, of excellence, would be incredible. But he was the first Black man to be a Formula 1 driver in a sport dominated by rich white men. The way he speaks, the way he carries himself, shows greatness, and he is a true trailblazer. And guess who was his coach? Yes, his father.

Both Serena Williams and Lewis Hamilton gained mastery and became the first to do something. This is what it means to be a trailblazer, and we are working on finding the trail you will make that is yours alone. Please notice that I want you to pursue your own curiosity, your own path, and build a life that is yours.

True trailblazers have a high tolerance for risk and failure, and the courage to create audacious goals and ideas. Once you achieve mastery in each area, you change your life and, yes, that of others. One book that made a substantial difference in my life is *Choose Yourself* by James Altucher. He discusses becoming an idea machine, something I loved learning to do and continue to this day. Writing ten ideas a day helped me further develop my creativity and willingness to try something new, and it will likely help you too.

One problem I looked at was the issue of immigration along the US–Mexico border. I asked, as a man that could have easily been a migrant father with his children, how can I help people escaping violence and poverty and climate adversity? How can I also solve problems for the United States so the government on this side of the border will help? The solution was to build an energy–water corridor along the border to create jobs, to provide water and clean energy, and to turn a region of danger and despair into prosperity and safety.

This was a crazy idea! But I worked at it, refining my ideas, building a team to solve the problem, and asking for guidance. And by taking a big, bold risk, I learned to be comfortable at the edge. One must be bold and confident, willing to take risks and be willing to fail—that, my friend, is what makes you a trailblazer! Once you do it, you can do it again and again—and the failures aren't what matter at all. When you're a trailblazer, you will continue forward, no matter what. And while my idea for the US–Mexico border has not become a reality as I originally envisioned it—yet, I have given many interviews and joined many diplomatic discussions about the complex issues and the border, as well as involved students in the process of addressing big, complex problems.

And this is where being a trailblazer really has meaning for me. Others can follow. Do you see my idea that becoming great, achieving mastery, is not about the goal? By finding your own desire, by taking risks, by using failure, you become a trailblazer, a person worth following—a mentor to others. And this is key to your Epic Life—you find you! What a gift, to find your true self, to find greatness in your gifts to the world! This is the Epic of Your Life!

Think of Muhammad Ali—"the Greatest"—one of the most significant athletes of the 20th century and likely the greatest heavyweight champion of all time. The man was a poet, civil rights activist, a man of God, a charismatic, witty individual. He was a true expert in boxing, but more than a boxer, he fought for equality for Black people by succeeding in the ring—he commanded the respect of white people in a time when Black men were undermined because of the color of their skin. With his charisma, his true excellence as a boxer, and his words, he brought our struggles against inequity to television.

I have written a lot about athletes, but many scientists are trailblazers too. For example, Marie Curie, often referred to as Madame Curie, was a Polish chemist and physicist who discovered polonium and radium. Radiation therapies used to treat cancer could not exist without these elements. She is known not only for being the first woman to win a Nobel Prize, but also for being the first person to win it twice. Madame Curie is a wonderful representation of a scientist, and her research saved millions of lives—a remarkable trailblazer; but first she achieved mastery as a chemist, then she became a trailblazer.

Eunice Newton Foote was an American scientist, inventor, and women's rights leader. In her home lab she demonstrated that CO_2 traps heat from the sun, which then causes our planet to warm, the phenomenon commonly referred to as the greenhouse effect. She was the first person to show by the greenhouse effect that high levels of CO_2 will lead to climate change.

Temple Grandin is on the autism spectrum, and as a child she struggled to learn language and to communicate with others. She found ways to work with her challenges, excel in her studies, and become a lauded professor of animal science. Temple developed technologies in animal science and even explained animal suffering. She became an animal rights advocate and a world-class professor. Her understanding of animal suffering stemmed from her learning to communicate effectively with others and overcoming her own challenges with autism. Her journey to become an illustrious scientist is indeed remarkable. She is a trailblazer!

Frederick Douglass is one of my heroes. He is a role model and big-time inspiration for me. He was born into slavery, learned to read, then fought for his freedom and then the freedom of others. He delivered lectures and speeches so beautiful and eloquent that people had a hard time believing he was once a slave with no formal education. His intellectual capacity and passion for the pursuit of justice for slaves and for women's rights and freedom speaks to me in a special way. He is believed to be the most photographed individual of the 19th century. He was an American abolitionist, orator, writer, publisher, and community leader. Mr. Douglass became the most important leader of the African American civil rights movement. He believed in personal development. He achieved freedom by acquiring knowledge and achieving mastery as a speaker and communicator. I urge you to study his life. For me, an individual that becomes a trailblazer in a way that betters the lives of others is indeed a person that shines with greatness. His work to fight for civil rights paved the way to freedom for many people of color and for women.

Nelson Mandela is another incredible man that I admire greatly. It is amazing that a person jailed for 27 years for advocating for the human rights of Black people in South Africa would later become the first president of South Africa, leading from 1994 to 1999. A man of great dignity, he led with wisdom and peace. The struggles and persistence of trailblazers in sports, science, politics, and other areas have changed humanity for the better.

Marcus Aurelius was a Roman emperor known for being a Stoic philosopher. (Stoic philosophy is a school of thought that emphasizes cultivating four cardinal virtues—wisdom, courage, temperance, and justice—and living in harmony with nature as the keys to a fulfilling life.) Stoic principles of moderation, humility, integrity, and equality helped him lead Rome into an era known as the Golden Age, despite dealing with the largest empire of his time and even a pandemic. He is a true trailblazer and one of my biggest heroes.

FACING UNCERTAINTY AND CHALLENGES

After mastering a gift you wish to share with the world, it is time to create, to discover the best ways to share that gift with the world. You can think of yourself as an artist or designer, someone that sees things from new angles. Figure out how to combine this new expertise with other skills of yours to solve problems, to effect positive change.

The fundamentals of stoicism helped me through a major life transition when I was working at Texas Tech University, but my oldest daughter needed a series of surgeries for a congenital condition. She needed to be in New York, where the best doctors were for her condition. Her mother, my second wife, and I were not getting along very well. We relocated to New York for the year, but inside, I knew I was not going back to Texas, and I also knew we were headed for divorce, but we focused on getting our baby healthy again.

Life at that time was so full of uncertainty, yet I remained calm and confident that everything was going to work out fine for my daughter and for my family. As I sat peacefully in upstate New York, I came up with dozens of ideas for how to move through the challenging situations—my daughter's medical condition, the end of my marriage.

It's important to dissect the challenging experiences to find the lesson or lessons within. This way, the next time we face something similar, we are wiser and better equipped than before.

I remember sitting in a sandwich shop texting a new colleague and friend from Purdue, Prof. Jay Gore, expecting to see him at an upcoming conference. He quickly replied that Purdue was hiring a named professor—and at that very moment, they were talking about me! The rest is history. Every time we fail at something there is a big opportunity to learn to become stronger; each setback moves us closer to achieving our goals. The year 2017 was one of the low points in my life. I lost a lot in the sale of our house in Texas. Yet, I was reinventing myself professionally, working hard on myself to make it happen. My family went through a dark and frightening time, but I was ready when an opportunity came along—and it turned out to be a good move not only for me, but for my daughter and my family.

Do not shy away from challenges and challenging moments; face them head on. Look at them as opportunities for learning and growth. Dig deep and persevere. Make time to do this, even when life's challenges might feel overwhelming. In the next chapters we will talk about some practical ways to stay focused.

For me, during that time in New York, I started thinking deeply about the US–Mexico border, and it turned out that this was the beginning of my career as a humanitarian engineer. I now tackle problems on climate change, social inequality, and climate adaptation—subjects on which today I am an authority, which has enabled me to help many people.

Choose to pursue meaningful personal goals with purpose. Do it passionately as if your life depends on it, because your life and the lives of others may depend on your courage to take action. You might not have thought about this before, but your actions can have a ripple effect, directly and indirectly, on humanity and your future. By becoming a trailblazer, you can change not only your own life, but the lives of your family, friends, community, and even the world! Dare to be a trailblazer!

CHAPTER SUMMARY

If you've made it this far, it's because deep down you know your life has a bigger purpose and in this chapter, I want to inspire you to take that brave leap into the unknown. I speak to you as someone who's walked that path: being a trailblazer isn't easy, but wow—what a powerful adventure it is! To be a trailblazer means daring to walk where there is no path, to think differently, and to leave a mark that others will one day follow.

Here I share the stories of giants like Arthur Ashe, Serena Williams, Lewis Hamilton, Muhammad Ali, Marie Curie, Temple Grandin, Frederick Douglass, and Nelson Mandela. They all broke barriers. What did they have in common? Courage, focus, and a burning desire to use their talent to transform their reality. They didn't wait for permission to be extraordinary. And neither should you.

I also open up about my own journey—how I shifted from being a traditional engineer to what I now call a "humanitarian engineer." A "crazy" idea about building an energy and water corridor along the U.S.–Mexico border ended up changing my entire professional path. I dared to dream, built a plan, brought a team together, and even though the idea didn't come to life exactly how I envisioned it, it opened doors I never imagined. That's when I realized that being a trailblazer isn't about reaching the top—it's about having the courage to begin.

Throughout this chapter, I talk about how I faced moments of deep uncertainty—from my eldest daughter's serious medical condition, to the breakdown of my second marriage, to starting over when I moved to Purdue. In the midst of all that chaos, I found peace by focusing on what truly mattered: my purpose, my family, my calling. Every challenge became a teacher. Every fall became fuel for growth.

To be a trailblazer is to take risks, to fail, to rise again, and to turn pain into purpose. It's about looking at the world and asking: "What can I contribute?" Because yes, you have something unique to offer!

The world needs your voice, your story, your ideas. And when you discover who you are and dare to live from that place of authenticity and courage—you become a true trailblazer!

So don't run from the hard stuff. Open your heart, create from hope, and take that first step. Remember: the future isn't written. You're writing it now.

CHAPTER ACTIVITY

ACTIVITY #7. Becoming a Trailblazer

Time needed: Approximately 15 minutes.

7a. Take a few minutes to clear your mind for the exercise. Lie down on your bed or sofa for 10 minutes. Just breathe calmly.

7b. How do you see yourself becoming a trailblazer? It can be in your work, personal, or community life.

RECOMMENDATIONS

Books

Originals: How Non-Conformists Move the World. Adam Grant. Viking, 2016. Shows how people who challenge the status quo can lead change, innovate, and transform industries without compromising their values.

Choose Yourself. James Altucher. CreateSpace, 2013. A modern manifesto on self-empowerment and the ability to reinvent oneself outside traditional systems like corporate jobs or formal education.

The Wim Hof Method. Wim Hof. Sounds True, 2020. The author shares his revolutionary approach to connecting mind and body through breathwork, cold exposure, and mindset—a path to self-mastery and mental/physical resilience.

Podcast

Huberman Lab. Hosted by Andrew Huberman (since 2021). The Stanford neuroscientist explores topics like neuroplasticity, mental health, sleep, and focus, offering practical tools to improve performance and everyday life.

Transformational Workshop

Unleash the Power Within. Tony Robbins. An intensive event that drives personal growth, breaks limiting fears, and awakens the trailblazing potential through movement, energy, and strategic vision.

Biography

Marie Curie: A Biography. Marilyn B. Ogilvie. Greenwood Press, 2004. The story of the first person to win two Nobel Prizes in different scientific fields. Her life is a symbol of courage, innovation, and discovery.

Movies

The Imitation Game. Dir. Morten Tyldum. The Weinstein Company, 2014. Tells the story of Alan Turing, whose mathematical genius helped crack the Enigma code and save millions during World War II.
Hidden Figures. Dir. Theodore Melfi. 20th Century Fox, 2016. An inspiring story of three African American women scientists at NASA who broke gender and racial barriers.

Works of Art

Liberty Leading the People, by Eugène Delacroix, 1830. Louvre Museum, Paris. An iconic painting representing revolutionary spirit, popular leadership, and the courage of those who rise against oppression.

Manifesto, by Julian Rosefeldt, 2015. Contemporary audiovisual installation. A multimedia artwork embodying the pioneering spirit through 13 artistic manifestos that challenge the status quo.

Woman Walking Through the Universe, by Joan Miró, 1960. Modern sculpture. https://publicdelivery.org/joan-miro-mural-mosaic-ceramic/. Represents human expansion into the unknown. A visual tribute to the trailblazing spirit.

7

Dare to Dream Big

The greater danger for most of us isn't that our aim is too high and we miss it, but that it is too low and we reach it.
—MICHELANGELO

Martin Luther King Jr. delivered a beautiful speech in which he urges young people to follow a blueprint for success in life, and he implores them to pursue something in life with excellence. Whether someone is a bricklayer or a janitor, do the job well with pride and excellence. In this chapter I lay out a plan that I have employed for many years for myself and with my graduate students. The method I share with you in this book has proven to be invaluable to me. If you choose to apply it to your life it can work for you too!

I have seen students unsure of how they want to apply their knowledge discover their gift after going through this process with me. It has been very rewarding for me to use this method to support students with autism or Asperger's, and those dealing with mental health challenges, and those students that came to work with me in the hope that one day they will complete their graduate work, or those who just came for a few weeks during the summer for a research experience. I am not saying that if you apply this method it will cure or correct an illness or issue, but it can help you develop a clear routine with specific action steps to achieve a better station in life, which will give you tools to handle those challenges in a better way. I say this because of my own challenges. This method helps me stay clam, centered, and focused.

Even as many of my students began their journey from high school to college with an application process that can feel very overwhelming, they are faced with the big questions, "What do you want to study?" and "Where do you want to attend college?" Then, four years later a similar question arises: "Are you going to get a job, or will you attend graduate school?"

Over the years, you see young adults repeatedly facing a similar issue, and many people come to a crossroads in their professional life at various points in their career. Then, as one moves through their life stages including nearing retirement age, one is often asked, "What are you going to do when you retire?" However, at retirement age, one's choices may be limited due to their neglecting their physical health. Many thought they would travel the world but realize since they can barely even walk a block, that may not be possible. Imagine that you work for 30 or 40 years and then you learn that you are not healthy enough to travel or even climb those beautiful mountains with a majestic view that takes your breath away. So even though I am mainly focusing this book on young adults, this method is of great value for people at all stages of life, since it can help you devise a plan to stay healthy or simply overcome a rough stage in life. It is critical for anyone including mature individuals.

In other cases, one's life "plan" changes due to divorce or the death of one's spouse. How do you take yourself from being "stuck" to a new, exciting stage in your life's journey? In this chapter, I will share with you many of these tools I learned from books and mentors and combined in a way that works for me. I recommend that you use the same strategy or at least go through the activities and try my method. Then, figure out which tools work best for you and use them regularly. In the end, this book's value lies in its usefulness to you on you taking action. I wrote this book intending to give you a blueprint to get yourself unstuck and build a life that is your masterpiece—however it looks in your dreams. I want to make sure that the life you live is *your life*, one that you designed, one that you feel proud of.

Blueprint Toward an Epic Life: Elite performers reach the top of their field by having a focused plan with measurable goals and activities. To get to the Olympics, a competitive swimmer has a non-negotiable daily schedule of distance and time to swim and a dietary plan that dictates fluid and nutrition intake. To achieve elite status in any field, a person must be consistent. They must keep up their training or actions over many hours, days, weeks, months, and years. There is no shortcut to achieve greatness or to build an Epic Life. In the next chapter, we will discuss tactics—the actions you need to take to reach these goals. In this chapter, you are building your focused goals and thinking strategically as you build a road map for your life. What are the directions that will take you toward your goals? What do you need to have along the way to ensure you reach those goals? Dare to dream a life worth fighting for, then put all of your heart and soul into it until you make it real. And that, my friend, is the gift you give to this beautiful world—this is your hero's journey that Josheph Campbell so eloquently talked about for decades—it is the Epic of Your Life!

It is now time to begin to build your road map for your life. Here are some of the components.

- *Goals:* Establish clear goals for the year, quarter, week, and day and read them each day. These goals are part of your blueprint.
- *Meditation:* Here we want to learn to relax the mind and be in a gratitude state so that the body, mind, and spirit are in sync.
- *Positive affirmations for your goals, your dream life:* Write them down, record your voice, create a vision board, and put affirmations in audio play. This gets you excited and builds confidence.

- *Quiet time:* Set aside 20 minutes every day to read, reflect, do breathing exercises, and/or just be in a state of silence. A few minutes to read a book that brings motivation or relaxation (e.g., the Bible) is part of this "Me Time."

Let's start with a fun activity—creating a "movie" from which you will pull your goals, a movie of your ideal life in the future.

Your Movie, Your Dream Life: Before you decide on areas for goals, let us play an imagination game. As children, we were good at creating fantasies in which we were the main character. Whether you were a knight slaying a dragon, a prima ballerina, a fighter pilot, a doctor, or any other amazing character, nothing was impossible!

> *If you don't like something, change it; if you can't change it, change your attitude.*
> —MAYA ANGELOU

CHAPTER SUMMARY

In this chapter, I invite you to do something powerful: to dream without limits. To dream like we did when we were kids and anything felt possible. I share with you—heart wide open—the method I've used for years with myself and my students: a blueprint for designing a life filled with purpose, clarity, and joy. Whether you're just starting out or entering a new season of life, this process is for everyone—because we all deserve to build an epic life.

Dreaming big is more than just setting goals—it's about committing to a vision that lights you up and gets you out of bed each morning with purpose. Here, I guide you through the first steps of that journey with intention. We start by building your personal life map: clear goals, actionable steps, and deep focus. But we don't stop there—we go inward too, strengthening your mind and spirit through daily meditation, affirmations, quiet time, and powerful visualization. This is your training to become the most vibrant version of yourself.

I walk you through creative exercises like writing your ideal life movie—engaging all your senses. Can you smell the sea air? Who's beside you? What kind of shape are you in? What passions light up your days? What change are you creating in the world? What's playing in the background—your favorite song? This process isn't just about dreaming—it's about turning that dream into reality, one inspired step at a time. Because when you align vision, action, and purpose . . . that's where the magic begins.

So, my friend, this chapter is your starting line. This is where the conscious design of your epic life begins. Dream big—and don't settle for anything less!

CHAPTER ACTIVITIES

ACTIVITY #8. Ideal Dream Life

Time needed: Approximately 20 minutes.

In this activity, the objective is to stay calm and excited about your ideal dream life. This activity will help you find, deep down inside of you, what matters to you and not the wishes of your parents or society. This is your own unique moment to dream a big audacious life.

8a. Suppose you get ten wishes for your life—with no limitations at all—two in each of these five categories: (1) Health; (2) Family and Friends; (3) Career or Business; (4) Finances or Wealth; and (5) Self-Mastery or Service. Write down each of these wishes. Now, just imagine you can write the screenplay for your ideal life using these wishes as reality. Remember, there are no limits here at all. Have the courage to dream big of how your ideal life is and be amazing in your movie. This is your best life, so take it seriously. Let yourself shine big time in this life! Remember that you are the main character and producer, and you get to do whatever you wish in your movie. Take as much time as needed to dream your life of no limits. Tune into your senses: See colors, smell the fragrance of flowers or the ocean, and hear the voices of your people. Can you hear your favorite inspiring song?

How do you project yourself to the world? As a calm, stoic person, or a fun-loving person full of passion?

Who is there with you?

Are you with friends? Family? Your children? How do they look? And how many do you have?

Are you helping communities in Africa? Underserved areas in your country? Are you helping the unhoused? Are you a person who stands for high moral standards?

Do you see your dream home? Does it have a pool? Do you have an amazing gym with a sauna, weights, and cold plunge?

What do you look like? What kind of physical shape are you in? How are you dressed?

Do you see your family? Either or both of your parents? How do they look? How many children?

Imagine your lifestyle. How are you dressed? What are your passions? Did you climb Mount Everest? Do you paint, or did you become a poet, writer, or singer? Did you discover something important in a lab?

How much money do you have in your savings? Where do you live? Are you the CEO of your company?

8b. Once you finish visualizing your ideal life, write it in your notebook. Keep writing, even if it is 20 pages long! Remember those 10 wishes. I want you to download your visions of your ideal life on paper. We are downloading the movie from your mind into a book to begin writing a road map—your masterpiece of a life!

ACTIVITY #9. Ideal Life Movie

Time needed: Approximately 20–30 minutes.

For this activity, it is important that you are relaxed and feel comfortable, in a mood to really let go of yourself and imagine a big, bold, exciting life. This activity is very critical as it will pave the way to determine your goals. If you are driving or doing anything else, stop it and lie down.

>   9a. In your notebook, write down your movie. Take as many pages as you need.

The characters, setting, and other details from the movie of your life will be used as a basis for creating your short-term and long-term goals. We will take it from the future into the present, and that is when the fun begins. By combining your goals with focused actions, with a clear plan and having faith that this is your destiny coming from within, you, my friend, will manifest your dream life into the present moment. In doing so, a beautiful being will emerge—trust me!

RECOMMENDATIONS

Books

The Dream Giver. Bruce Wilkinson. Multnomah, 2003. A modern parable that invites you to step out of your comfort zone and follow the call of your dreams.

The Alchemist. Paulo Coelho. HarperOne, 1988. A spiritual story about a young shepherd who follows the signs of the universe in search of his personal legend.

Big Magic: Creative Living Beyond Fear. Elizabeth Gilbert. Riverhead Books, 2015. A guide to releasing your creativity and living with courage—without letting fear limit your authentic expression.

The Neverending Story. Michael Ende. Thienemann, 1979. A fantasy novel that explores the transformative power of imagination and self-belief.

You Are Stronger Than You Think. Joel Osteen. FaithWords, 2021. A message of faith, hope, and inner strength for those who dare to dream bigger.

The Magic of Thinking Big. David J. Schwartz. Touchstone, 1987 reprint. A timeless classic offering strategies to expand your personal vision and achieve meaningful goals.

Goals! Brian Tracy. MJF Books, 2010. A practical manual on how to set and achieve ambitious personal goals with focus and discipline.

Biographies

Martin Luther King Jr.: A Life—Marshall Frady. Penguin Books, 2002. An intimate look into the life of the civil rights leader whose dream of equality changed history.

I Am Malala. Malala Yousafzai. Little, Brown and Company, 2013. The courageous story of a young girl who defended her right to dream of education for all.

Walt Disney: The Triumph of the American Imagination. Neal Gabler. Knopf, 2006. A portrait of the man who created a universe where dreams come true and imagination has no limits.

Courage to Soar. Simone Biles. Zondervan, 2016. The story of how the Olympic gymnast overcame physical and emotional obstacles to elevate her life beyond the imaginable.

Movies

The Secret Life of Walter Mitty. Dir. Ben Stiller. 20th Century Fox, 2013. A shy office worker embarks on an epic adventure that transforms how he sees himself and the world.

Inception. Dir. Christopher Nolan. Warner Bros., 2010. A psychological thriller exploring the layered nature of dreams and their creative and destructive power.

Billy Elliot. Dir. Stephen Daldry. Working Title Films, 2000. A working-class boy fights for his right to dance ballet in a conservative, male-dominated environment.

Soul. Dir. Pete Docter. Pixar, 2020. An animated reflection on purpose, dreams, and what it really means to "live."

October Sky. Dir. Joe Johnston. Universal Pictures, 1999. Based on a true story, a young man escapes his mining-town destiny by building rockets and reaching for the stars.

Works of Art

Dream of a Sunday Afternoon in the Alameda Central, by Diego Rivera, 1947. Museo Mural Diego Rivera, Mexico City. A mural representing Mexico's past, present, and future with dreamlike and revolutionary figures.

The Garden of Earthly Delights, by Hieronymus Bosch, c. 1490–1510. Prado Museum, Madrid. An enigmatic work reflecting human dreams, pleasures, and the consequences of desire.

Morning Star, by Joan Miró, 1940. Fundación Miró. A surrealist painting capturing the essence of the dream world and cosmic imagination.

Water Lilies, by Claude Monet. Series created between 1897–1926. Musée de l'Orangerie, Paris. Represents the inner world, contemplation, and the invisible beauty that nourishes the dreaming soul.

Plans for the Ideal City, by Leonardo da Vinci, c. 1487. A futuristic Renaissance vision of urbanism: functional, beautiful, and visionary. A utopia of its time.

8

Designing Your Epic Year

When there is no vision, the people perish.
—PROVERBS 29:18, KING JAMES BIBLE

G oals are the landmarks and signposts on your road map to your Epic Life. But the best thing about striving to reach your goals is the person you become along the way. Go back to those 10 wishes and these 5 pillars: (1) Health; (2) Family and Friends; (3) Career or Business; (4) Finances; and (5) Self-Mastery or Service. These are fundamental values in an Epic Life; the first four might seem obvious, and the fifth may be the most important. We're going to keep those in mind as we take your "movie" and translate it into goals and subgoals such that you have a clear road map all the way to daily action.

In this chapter, you'll replay the movie and think carefully about who is in your ideal life, how you are spending your time, and who you are as a person. Then you'll write down goals that are steps to reach that ideal life that you projected in the previous chapter. You might not have any idea how to get there from where you are today—that's where all the mentors and role models and books come in, and your planning comes in. Ask others who went before you, and don't stop trying, ever.

For example, if you envision yourself in the future studying primates in the jungle like Jane Goodall, you will need to figure out what career that is, how people train for that, which university will be a good fit for you, how to fund your education, and so on. You'll also need to be in very good physical shape to be able to handle long hours of walking and climbing in the jungle. And if you want a partner, you'll need to seek someone who wants to live the same kind of life, or you will need to agree to spend a lot of time apart. All of these things have many "mini goals" or sub-goals that are completed as part of your months, weeks, or daily actions.

> *A good goal is like a strenuous exercise—it makes*
> *you stretch.*
> —MARY KAY ASH

Goals: Setting Action Plans

A person who is aligned physically, mentally, and spiritually is more resilient, making it easier to handle challenges. Your health is the most important gift you have, so please take it seriously. In a healthy body a brain can function better. When you are spiritually in a good state you become a better person—a person that naturally cares more about others and feels this sense of peace. When you have a positive mindset, you care more about maintaining a healthy body, and your attitude toward the world in general improves. It's a virtual feedback loop.

If you achieve mastery of yourself over a lifetime, you, my friend, achieve greatness. Let me explain. For example, if you learn how to optimize your eating habits so that you maximize your energy and well-being as an adult, you become more productive and full of life. In the same way, learning how to rest, take proper vitamins and proper hydration, practice meditation and exercise like yoga such that your mind and body are functioning well, then you are achieving self-mastery. And this is

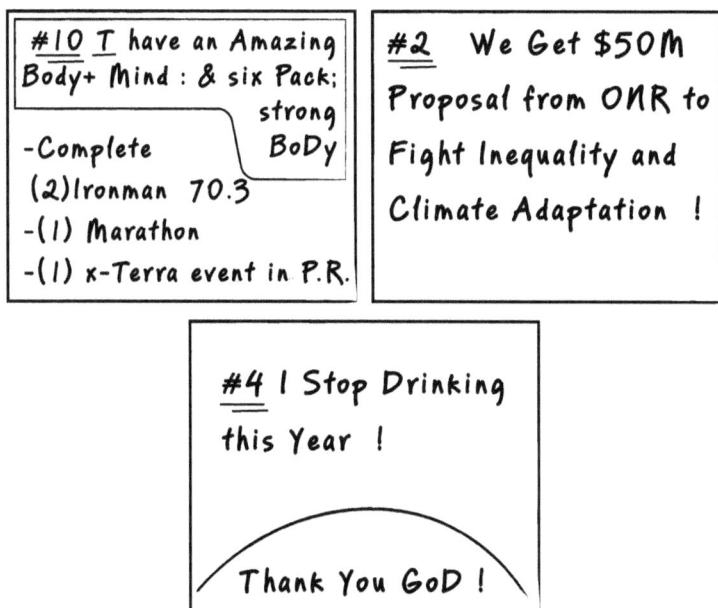

#10 I have an Amazing Body+ Mind : & six Pack; strong BoDy
-Complete (2) Ironman 70.3
-(1) Marathon
-(1) x-Terra event in P.R.

#2 We Get $50M Proposal from ONR to Fight Inequality and Climate Adaptation !

#4 I Stop Drinking this Year !

Thank You GoD !

Figure 2. Examples of goals for Mastery/Health and Career that you place around your home to view every single day. Each goal is written in the present tense and is positive. These are examples of yearly goals. On Goals #10, I put some key action plans: Complete two Ironman 70.3, a marathon, and another triathlon X-Terra.

what I am talking about here. Each day, the goal is to grow a bit more than yesterday, to stay in optimum physical, mental, and spiritual health, and to build action plans that improve your relationships with yourself, with your family, with your friends, with your community; and to build healthy finances so you can live a full and happy life. Even when you have made all those good habits, you will have setbacks. However, you will have a solid foundation to support you, and you will have a resilient mind and body to overcome those difficult moments when they show up.

These five pillars are designed to sustain your Epic Life. At the core is how to manage yourself and grow as an individual each day, and how you handle setbacks that determine your progress in Life. Some people do not need to add an item for goals on Self-Mastery, so they can then include Service or any other value that matters big time to you. This may include service to your church, service to your community, or service to your profession. You can just add one more pillar, but I recommend you keep them at a maximum of five pillars.

Generally speaking, self-mastery is building habits that will help you master who you are and where you are going, while improving daily. If you went to college, do not think for one minute that you are done learning, that once you earn a college degree, if that is one of the goals you wish for, that you are done, or if you landed your dream job or if you are a maestro in music, you made it. Not at all; you're just getting started.

So, here in Self-Mastery, selecting a skill, a hobby, or just learning every day is sufficient. You can learn about trading, or a new language, or public speaking. "Service." It is about giving to others; it is sharing what you are learning with others, it is not just giving with money. Giving your time, a hug, a smile, or love is greater than money when someone is hurting for that human connection. Service could be volunteer work you do for your profession or community, people you mentor, or paying a medical bill for a family in need.

YEAR 1 GOALS

Since you wrote down 10–20 goals per area you have anywhere from 50 to 100 goals written down. In this section you will edit the list to select your top 10 goals for Year 1. This is about two goals per area: Health, Finances, Family and Friends, Self-Mastery or Service, and Career. And then from those 10 goals, you will determine your epic goal for the year—this is the goal that will be a major game changer in your life if you achieve it this year and will transform your life!

Remember to write each goal in the present tense, as if it is already happening. Keep it positive and specific. For example, "I complete a successful triathlon 70.3 in Puerto Rico by March 16 of 2025 under

7 hours." A 70.3 triathlon is a sport event in which you swim 1.2 miles, run 13.1 miles, and bike 56 miles, all in one day. Notice that your goal is present tense (I complete), positive (a successful triathlon), and specific (date, hours, and location).

For another example, if you want to lose 20 pounds, then write it as "I lose 20 pounds by the end of March." For each area, ask yourself the following question: "Which goals, if I achieve them, could be a game changer or will make things better, easier for me?" This filter is sifting through your goals looking for one that could positively impact your life for the better. For example, if you suffer from anxiety, develop a strategy for controlling that and learn how to manage yourself such that when you know you are becoming anxious you know what to do, or better yet, develop a solid plan to keep your body-mind-spirit in sync and healthy so you do not become anxious. So now, let's say that you initially had 20 goals in a category, but let's start by reducing the list to your top three to five goals per category.

Mark the goals that could change your life big time with three stars. They should be part of the short list. Aim to have 3–5 per area. You will learn to focus on things that matter, and please learn that your health is part of your wealth—treasure your health. In my pillar, I always put my Health first, and noticed that it is not just body health. I am also talking about your brain health (e.g., please see these references for brain health at the end of the chapter) and your spiritual health.

Then, which goals are short-term goals, ones that can be completed in 6 to 12 months? Select 1–2 goals. With your big-time goals and your short-term goals, you should have a maximum of 10 goals for Year One.

Then, which are mid-term goals, ones that will likely take two to three years to achieve? Do not worry about how many mid-term goals you have; normally I keep about three goals for 2–3 years. Which are long-term goals for beyond five years? In my case I have 1–2 goals for the long term. Just set these aside for now.

Year One of Your Epic Life: Now you have 10 goals for your first year. Some are life-changing, "big-time" goals; others are short-term,

10 Goals Selection (50–100 Goals): What Matters Big Time?

Filtering the Noise from What Really Matters!

For each area, ask yourself the following question: "Which goals, if I achieve them, could be a game changer or will make things better, easier for me?" This filter is sifting through your goals looking for those that could potentially change your life for the better.

Which goals are you passionate about and excited to achieve? Why? Highlight those game-changer goals in green. For those in green, number each goal in terms of years.

1. Short-term goals to complete in 1 year. Which goals are short-term goals from 6 to 12 months (1)?
2. Mid-term goals from 2 to 3 years (3).
3. Long-term goals for beyond 5 years (5).

For the first year, you should end up with 1–2 goals for each area, so you have about 8–10 goals to work toward.

Look at 1–3 goals as mid-term goals and 1–2 goals as long-term goals. These goals are for each area, which means that you will now have a set of goals in areas you can use to build a solid blueprint.

Some goals definitely will take more than 12 months to achieve (e.g. 5 to 10 years).

relatively achievable goals. Of these, *which is the one goal that could be the biggest game changer in your life*? That goal is your #1. Label it "My Epic Goal." Then look at the list of longer-term goals. Which one will transform your life? That goal is "My Masterpiece Goal." Your masterpiece goal (it is your vision in your life—like a purpose) will define the

#5 I am an Amazing Father	My EPIC GOAL
· Strong & Loving · Listen to Khall & Girls · Very Supportive · WoW Moments w. them	#1 We Receive $93M from HUD for Converting UPRB & 5-schools to 100% Renewable Energy and Power 20-Electric Buses for the children !

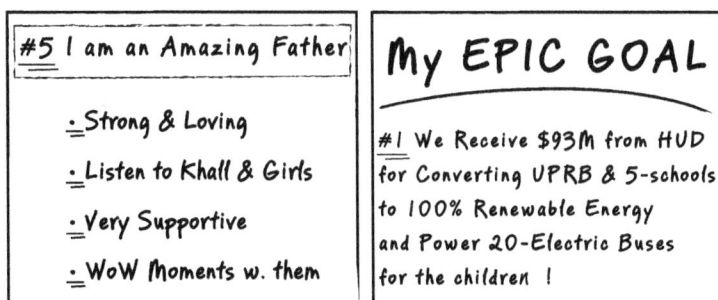

Figure 3. Example of a Family goal and a major goal for the year. I call it "My Epic Goal" of the year. If I achieve it, my life will change drastically for the better.

way you work on mid-term and short-term goals. Later we will talk in more depth about finding that purpose. For now, do not worry about making everything align. I want you to focus on Year One and to learn to do this process and see the transformation in your life. As you keep doing this process and learning what works best for you, eventually all of this will be natural for you. Also, friends, there are times in your year when a crisis happens, so it is okay to adjust your goals and time-lines, but never give up.

Write these goals in your notebook, put them in your computer, put them on the walls of your home (well, your spouse or partner may not like it, so in your bedroom or closet will be fine too). And now we will create your vision board of that dream life of yours. Surround yourself with constant reminders of your goals that will get you to your Epic Life!

MY VISION BOARD

Remember your movie? Now, let's have fun finding pictures of your ideal life and putting that beautiful life of yours on a board that we call your vision board. Friends, having your goals in front of you and then having a private place that you visit often in your house where you can see your ideal life illustrated—this will motivate you and push you to take action every day. This is a constant reminder of where you are going and why today you will grow a bit more or walk an extra mile or call one more potential customer or just approach that person that you like very much.

Some of your mid-term, long-term, and short-term goals should be there. Remember, nobody is "lucky." Successful businesses build a road map; universities have a strategic plan. The CEO has strategic planning for investors and uses it to guide decision making. Remember, when you go on a long trip, you need a specific address to aim for to begin your trip, right? Otherwise, you go nowhere. Goals and a vision give you direction and fuel you with excitement and passion to keep going.

SPECIFIC ACTION PLAN FOR EACH GOAL

We are now going to write specific action plans for each goal (3–5 short steps / action items needed to achieve each goal, see figures 2 and 3) and think about why each goal is so important to you. For example, if your goal is to go to a top university but without debt, then you need to build some action plans: (1) Identify key requirements for admission. (2) Which universities are top in your field? (3) What opportunities for fellowships do they have? (4) Will you save some funds to cover college costs, or will you need to work, or will you join the armed forces so they pay for your college, or will you ask a rich relative to fund you? There are many alternatives, including visiting the universities, talking with professors, or looking for foundations for funding or fellowships. In this scenario, I urge you to visit those institutions and talk with staff and faculty. Many times, wealthy private universities have such a big endowment that students are surprised by the resources available for them. Never disregard a private expensive university; they could give you a full ride.

Quarterly Calendar Goals: Are we done? Not yet! We need to make goals for the year in the present tense and specific, and then take action every day, every week, every month, and every quarter to achieve them!

Buy a 90-day wall calendar (approximately 36″ × 24″; see the example in figure 4) on which you can write in the days and months. I know some of you prefer to use a digital calendar, but it will be helpful to also create a physical calendar (OfficeMax, Office Depot, Staples, and Amazon sell them for about $21). The physical calendar allows you to clearly write down your quarterly goals and see them daily on your wall. Writing, then looking regularly at your goals helps your brain to imprint them. It is also a great way to monitor your daily progress on the action steps, and yet see the long-term (90 days) path ahead.

I have my 90-day calendar in my walk-in closet. Every time I go to my closet, I see my goals for the quarter (about five subgoals that are related to my yearly goals), and any specific events or goals for the month (birthdays, major events, dateline for proposal or project, dateline for a sports event, etc.). Notice that within a month I focus on different items of my five areas. These areas represent items I value in my life.

In the example shown in figure 4, in April my focus is on my family and on getting my daughter healthier. In May, my focus is on a family vacation. In June my focus shifts to my Summer Institute (areas of focus are on Service to others). In June I work on climate change problems with young students and on mentoring. Basically, in the summers, I work on helping young people find opportunities to further grow their careers and enter college. Do you see that every month I changed my focus depending on the pressing issues and goals? You need to be flexible as life throws you some curves. This system allows me to remain focused on my important goals while being flexible so I can adjust when necessary. Also, you are constantly monitoring your progress as you know what you are doing every month and week.

Charles Darwin wrote, "It is not the strongest of the species that survives but the one willing to adapt." We need to be adaptable—learn to be a resilient person!

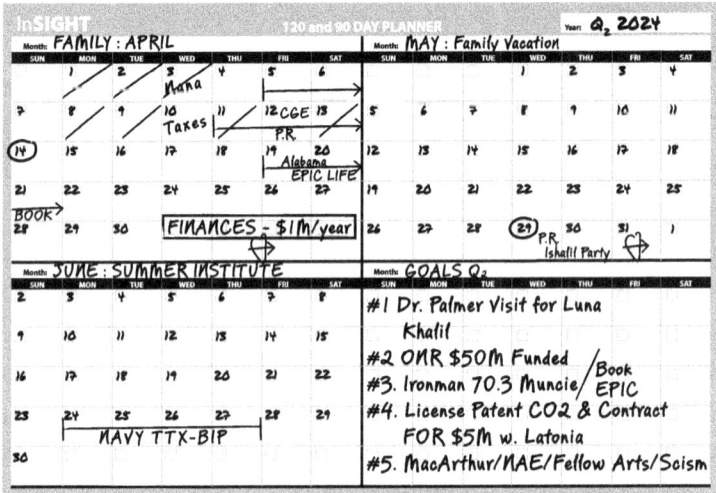

Figure 4. A 90-day calendar with key focus area and 5 goals/subgoals.

Creating Your Calendar: At the top of the 90-day calendar, fill in the quarter and year. In figure 4, I put Q2 2024 on the top right-hand side, then the months: April, May, and June. Next to the name of each month, put a key major focus (e.g., Family, Career, Health, Mastery, Finances, etc.) or outcome. If during that time a crisis arises, you may have to alter your quarterly action plan drastically, but do not give up on your goals for the year. It's important to remain on track but be flexible.

For example, maybe Grandma went to the hospital for a big surgery. Or, in my case, my ex-wife and I had to drop everything and devote our attention to our daughter when she became ill. My focus and subgoals for the quarter may change but my long-term strategy continues. She was able to overcome her health challenges, and I was able to remain strong and steady and on track for my year.

At the bottom right of the calendar, I put down 5 key goals (in most cases these are subgoals of your yearly goals) for that quarter that align with my top 10 goals and include my epic goal of the year. Remember, the epic goal is the one that, if completed, will change your life big time!

If you do not achieve your goals, at the end of the year during your reflection time, ask yourself what new changes you will make. Sometimes, when working on your quarter some goals are achieved and some others not exactly. It is okay; modify them a bit for next quarter and then add/modify your next subgoals for the following quarter. You are constantly acting and using your feedback (reflection) to adjust your next steps.

Now begin to fill in some subgoals. For example, if you are saving money for a trip to Hawaii, you need to take aggressive action toward your saving plan. If the goal is to go on vacation to Hawaii with the family next summer, you calculate that it will cost you $10K. The subgoal is then the actions you need to take to accomplish that goal. Thus, a subgoal is "I save $2K per month for the next five months." Then, ask yourself what you will do to get $2K per month. This could be a part-time job or tutoring or consulting. Thus, a clear actionable subgoal could be: "I tutor five students per week, and I enjoy the difference I make in their life." Think about it. You have a clear subgoal and know when you start; you also enjoy touching their lives. If you charge each one $100 per hour, you have $500 per week and thus $2K per month. Then, how will you get the five clients? This, my friend, is how you create an action plan to meet your goal of going to Hawaii. Your goals are not dreams; they help you build a path, a road map for your life.

WEEKLY GOALS

We have a focus area related to each monthly goal, but don't lose sight of the other areas: (1) Health; (2) Career and Business; (3) Self-Mastery or Service; (4) Finances; and (5) Family and Friends. All we need is consistent attention to ensure your overall life is solid. Your core priority on a given day or week will change to achieve your key activities for the week. I spend 10–20 minutes in the morning planning my day and thinking of my previous week. Then, I start to think about what my focus will be next week. What goals are important for me to achieve so that if I complete them they will make a big impact for the quarter? For example, using the example before of the $2K per month, perhaps next week I may focus on creating flyers, or creating a social media account to promote my tutoring services, or I tell friends, or simply go to a school and tell them about my services and credentials. These are clear actions to get my five customers.

So, in preparation for my new week, I ask myself:

- What are the most valuable things I can do this week that will make a big impact for the month?

Asking how valuable those activities are will help you set the focus of your week on what really matters. Basically, you will spend effort on activities that will propel you forward big time. I also check to see what I missed the previous week that was very important and needs to be carried forward. Notice that my goal for the week is to achieve one or two of my most important goals. We do not have to-do lists! When you complete them, celebrate your achievements. If you don't reach your target, it's okay, but do what you can to keep the forward momentum going. Looking at your vision board reminds you of the movie you created of your masterpiece life. Looking at your yearly goals tells you what must be achieved that year, and the quarterly calendar further narrows your activities by month. You think of the long-term but the action is in the now.

DAILY GOALS

As shown in figure 4, you will see that I have 4–5 key categories that I focus on every day and every week: (1) Career; (2) Health and Fitness; (3) Self-Mastery, and so on. I use color to help me stay focused on big items each week, and for each day, the asterisk next to items means they are super important things that will advance my weekly and yearly goals big time. By now you can see that nothing in the creation of an Epic Life is luck! To the day, to the hour, you know what you are doing. Your daily actions support your weekly plans, and your weekly plans support your monthly subgoals, which in turn support your quarterly outcomes; your quarterly goals support your yearly goals and your yearly goals, the long-term goals! This, my friend, is a road map, and you do this all the time in your life. When you have a life like this, you are working for your long-term progress. "If you don't do this, my friend, you are working for somebody else's dream"—this is plain and simple.

I learned a lot about goal setting, planning, and how to focus my efforts from several key books: *Goals!* by Brian Tracy, *The One Thing* by Gary Keller, and *The 10X Rule* by Grant Cardone. There are other good books from Zig Ziglar, such as *See You at the Top*, that are important to read also. Over the years, I modified my own approach and my way of doing things to get it down to the level described in this chapter, which I think is very effective. This approach could accelerate your own results big time! If you can focus, you can achieve every three months what the average person achieves in one year. When you do this, you build a routine for your life. As I mentioned earlier, remember to read or listen to something positive, uplifting, with positive messaging every day. You can create surroundings in your own home that support your dreams and goals, and your well-being (e.g., mental peace). While this may sound like a lot to do, it is not. This approach, however, takes focus and deliberate action toward achieving your ideal life—by focusing on activities that matter because they support your goals and you accelerate your daily progress!

CHAPTER SUMMARY

When you work aggressively on your goals and key subgoals every month, along with dates and target actions (hire a weight training coach, sign up for yoga class, register for a finance certification or a cooking class, go to a workshop on nutrition, etc.), you know that you are taking action. Sometimes, however, the action you take does not yield the desired result, which means that you need to take a different approach to reach your goal. This is okay; this is why resilience and reflection are important. The key is to keep improving and never give up on your masterpiece.

> *The two most important days in your life are the day*
> *you are born and the day you find out why.*
> —MARK TWAIN

Here are the key must-do activities to keep you moving toward building an epic year:

Vision Board: Display photos of your ideal life as you saw it in your movie. Record your voice saying aloud your goals for the year. Be excited and say it with passion as if the goals have already been reached. Be happy in the recording and show a voice of positivity!

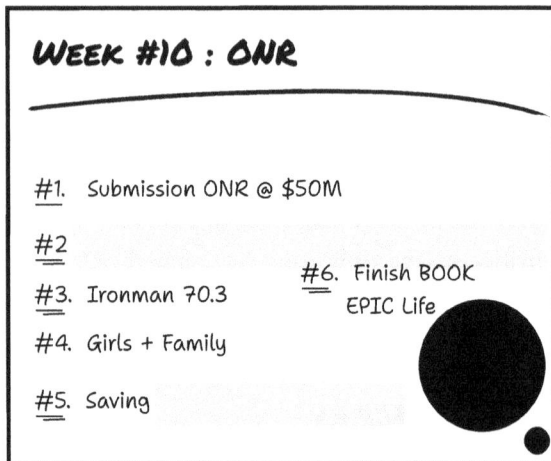

Figure 5. Board with key weekly goals. This is a major focus for you.

Yearly Goals: 8–10 goals: Why + action strategy (just 3 to 4 bullets of key actions as shown in Figure 3).

Quarterly Goals: 12 weeks plan and subgoals for each month.

Weekly Goals: Each week of the 90 days calendar (12 weeks in total) will show key focus activities and calculated action steps. For example, on Week #1, write key subgoals and focused action items for that week. Put the key focus of that week on a white or black board.

Daily Goals: This is not a to-do list. Daily goals focus on key activities related to weekly, monthly, and quarterly goals to reach your vision and purpose in life.

CHAPTER ACTIVITIES

ACTIVITY #10. Health: Body-Mind-Spirit

Time needed: Approximately 10–15 minutes. In Health I include your physical body, your mind, and your spiritual development. When those three areas are solid and in sync, you will feel amazing and at peace.

10a. Using details from the movie of your life you created in the last activity of chapter 7, write down 10–20 goals to describe your ideal physical and mental health. Be specific; write as much detail as you want. Is your heart happy? Are you in good physical shape? Are you running a marathon? Are you training to climb Mount Everest? Did you master a new style of martial arts? Join a fun sports league? Do you have any bad habits, like smoking or excessive drinking? Think big and try to download all the descriptions of physical and mental well-being that you wrote down in the previous chapter.

This is the first time I've mentioned destructive habits like smoking or other addictions. When we have addictions, we are enslaved, and you must be a free individual in every single way to build your Epic Life. If you are struggling with addictions of any kind, address this with whatever kind of help you need, like joining a support group or detox clinical. This is very important, and a goal in this area is critical to include.

ACTIVITY #11. Family and Friends

Time needed: Approximately 10–15 minutes. You will write 10–20 goals in this area.

11a. Again, from the movie of your life in chapter 7, write down 10–20 goals that are related to your family and friends. Who is in your life? Are you married, do you have a life partner, are you in a nontraditional relationship? Do you have children? Are extended family members nearby? Do you have valued relationships with coworkers or colleagues? How do you spend time with others—do you have family gatherings, take vacations with friends, travel the world with a group of researchers on an expedition? Are you in the movie with a friend who is not currently in your life? Write a goal for resuming that relationship if that is important to your happiness. How is your relationship with the people you love? Sometimes, making a goal to call your parents for 10 minutes once a week will make a difference in your relationship with them. Or, taking your significant other on a simple road trip will improve your relationship with them for the better. Remember, write goals that are important and valuable to you, not what others might expect of you.

ACTIVITY #12. Finances

Time needed: Approximately 15 minutes. As with the other categories, identify 10–20 goals in this category that are related to finances. It's not enough to simply say "I want to make enough to be comfortable" or "I want to be rich." You need to be specific about the details of your masterpiece, so you can make decisions that align with your true burning desire and feel right to you. For example, I earn $1 million by the end of the year 2025.

12a. Are you living in a mansion or driving around the United States or Europe in an RV? Do you live in a major international city, a small town, a rural area, or a suburb? Do you need to pay for education? What do you buy and own—cars, clothes, furniture? You may dream of living in a large house with terraces overlooking the ocean and envision yourself hosting a formal party. Or are you in a small, beautiful house in the countryside, maybe even one that you built with your own hands? You may have chickens, pets, or a special place for your bikes. Your amazing life is for you to define, ignoring outside influences of societal or parental expectations, mainstream media, or pressure from peers. How much money do you earn? Be clear about how much money you have in your savings in addition to what you bring in each year. Do you live from your investments or your business?

Having large debt is not epic; it restricts your freedom. Be specific in your goals! Think of using GPS while driving: You need to enter the precise information of the location where you want to end up. Your blueprint for an Epic Life must be clear and specific so your mind knows where to go. Are you paying off student or car loans? Do you want to save up to buy your dream sports car, or do you want to save enough money to take a year off to travel the world? How much will that cost you? How much money do you have for an emergency (typically a minimum of six months of monthly expenses)? What are your assets worth? Do you have a car (color, make, model), a boat, multiple homes? As before, write at least 10 goals for your finances and wealth.

ACTIVITY #13. Career or Business

Time needed: Approximately 10 minutes. How do you see yourself contributing to society? Does the work that you do help make our world a better place? Are you happy and focused? Do you see yourself in a state of blessing in a job that brings you joy and pays a fair salary? What would you like to achieve in your profession? Do you want to be an executive at your company?

13a. Write 10 to 20 career goals, being as specific as you can. Is your goal to get more education, or maybe have more freedom in a role that allows you to work from home so that you can play with your kids more or exercise more? Will your career be raising kids as a stay-at-home spouse? Is your goal to become the top salesperson in your company? Think back to your movie. What kind of impact and value do you bring to others in your profession? Do you see yourself expressing a unique gift and getting paid for giving it to the world? Is the work you do for a humanitarian cause? Do you see yourself using your courage in doing something unique in your career or a company/startup that you co-founded?

Remember, the goals you write are to help you improve who you are as a person and ultimately to contribute to society. If you wrote 20 goals per area up to this point, you are already looking at 80 goals! Good news: When this is all pulled together, you will choose your top goals, and you will also see that there will be overlap in how you reach some of them.

ACTIVITY #14. Self- Mastery or Service

Time needed: Approximately 10–15 minutes.

14a. From your dream life, select some activities that you can identify as Self-Mastery or Service, then write 10–20 goals related to them.

RECOMMENDATIONS

Books

Atomic Habits. James Clear. Avery, 2018. A proven method for building powerful habits that transform your daily life.

The 7 Habits of Highly Effective People. Stephen R. Covey. Free Press, 1989. A comprehensive guide to personal effectiveness, based on timeless principles.

Essentialism. Greg McKeown. Crown Business, 2014. Teaches how to focus on what truly matters and eliminate the non-essential to live with purpose.

The Power of Full Engagement. Jim Loehr & Tony Schwartz. Free Press, 2003. Shifts the focus from time management to energy management for sustainable performance.

Designing Your Life. Bill Burnett & Dave Evans. Knopf, 2016. A design-thinking approach to building a meaningful life aligned with your values.

The End of Mental Illness. Daniel G. Amen. Tyndale Refresh, 2020. A neuroscientific vision for healing, preventing, and transforming mental health.

The 10X Rule. Grant Cardone. Wiley, 2011. A call to multiply your goals and actions to achieve extraordinary results.

Become a Better You. Joel Osteen. Howard Books, reprint 2009. Spiritual inspiration to live with more faith, hope, and greatness.

You Can, You Will. Joel Osteen. FaithWords, reprint 2015. A motivational message to activate the potential within you.

Brain Energy. Christopher M. Palmer. BenBella Books, 2022. How metabolic health impacts your mind, performance, and ability to reinvent yourself.

The Body Keeps the Score. Bessel van der Kolk. Penguin Books, 2015. Reveals how trauma affects the body and how to heal it to reclaim your personal power.

See You at the Top. Zig Ziglar. Pelican Publishing, 2000; 25th edition. A self-help classic on how a positive attitude and determined action can take you to the top.

Biographies

Benjamin Franklin: An American Life. Walter Isaacson. Simon & Schuster, 2003. The example of someone who designed his time, habits, and legacy with intention and wisdom.

Oprah: A Biography. Kitty Kelley. Crown Publishing Group, 2010. The story of how Oprah built her empire with authenticity, vision, and resilience.

Total Recall. Arnold Schwarzenegger. Simon & Schuster, 2012. From Austria to Hollywood, he narrates how he designed each stage of his life with vision, discipline, and ambition.

Becoming. Michelle Obama. Crown Publishing Group, 2018. A testimony of planning, reinvention, and authenticity through service and self-overcoming.

Movies

Groundhog Day. Dir. Harold Ramis. Columbia Pictures, 1993. A man lives the same day over and over—until he decides to redesign it. A parable about transformation through the ordinary.

Yes Man. Dir. Peyton Reed. Warner Bros., 2008. A comedy about saying "yes" to new opportunities and escaping autopilot.

About Time. Dir. Richard Curtis. Universal Pictures, 2013. A charming story about how to use time with purpose and redesign your life with love and intention.

The Intern. Dir. Nancy Meyers. Warner Bros., 2015. Reinventing oneself at any age. A message about purpose, experience, and second chances.

Works of Art

The Creation of Adam, by Michelangelo. Sistine Chapel, 1511. A symbolic image of creation: the spark of life, purpose, and the beginning of something epic.

The Compass Rose (classic nautical design, 14th–15th centuries). A symbol of direction, focus, and guidance for your journey.

The Aztec Calendar (Sun Stone). National Museum of Anthropology, Mexico, 15th century. An ancestral vision of time as cyclical energy—perfect for beginning a new chapter with intention.

Leonardo da Vinci's Sketches, c. 1487–1519. Drawings of machines, cities, and the human body as metaphors of conscious and limitless human design.

Tibetan Mandalas (Buddhist ritual art), 12th century to present. Visual representations of cosmic order and inner harmony. Tools for meditating, focusing, and envisioning your epic year.

9

A Daily Routine

Faith in Action

*Winning is not a sometime thing; it's an all-time
thing. You don't win once in a while, you don't do
things right once in a while, you do them right all the
time. Winning is a habit. Unfortunately, so is losing.*
—VINCE LOMBARDI

"Faith in action" is living out your plans. You wrote your goals (by
years, quarters, months, weeks, and days), you built your vision
board, identified your epic goal for the year, and created a movie
of your ideal life. You may ask, "What else can I do to accelerate the
attainment of my goals?" In this chapter we will build a daily routine
that will help accelerate your growth and help you move faster toward
achieving your Epic Life. Consistency, doing things daily, helps you
build strong discipline and will move you toward the goals you set
in chapter 8—and yes, toward self-mastery too. A person with discipline can achieve anything in life!

Look at the lives of many successful people. Many of them were "not
supposed to be there" (e.g., were too short, not a genius, too poor, had

the wrong upbringing, etc.). For example, the great Oprah Winfrey grew up in the South during times of major discrimination, endured sexual abuse as a child, and overcame poverty to become a highly respected talk show host and billionaire. Michael Jordan did not make the varsity high school basketball team when he tried out as a sophomore. Go to the NICU at any hospital and you will see little babies beating the odds who go on to become amazing individuals.

A daily habit is like a turbocharger in a car—it will accelerate your progress big time, and you will become a performance machine. Notice that in key areas (values; the five pillars) we have: (1) Health; (2) Finances or Wealth; (3) Family and Friends; (4) Self-Mastery or Service; and (5) Career or Business. I work on these core values every day—but I don't have to think that hard about it every day, because I've built habits into my regular routines that move me step-by-step toward my goals and keep me aligned with my five pillars.

To build a masterpiece life, you must build a daily routine to execute your plan for an epic day, then epic weeks, epic months, and epic years—no compromises here! Leave nothing to "luck." You build a blueprint to achieve your goals and then you do the work, but all is done on a solid system of a daily routine, which will help build habits. If you build a startup, isn't that what you build for your company—a business plan, a clear road map to keep things on track and guide your team to focus on what matters? You are the CEO of your Epic Life—and nobody cares more about your life than you! So, take it seriously because it is your life. Think of McDonald's, one of the most successful franchises of all time. Do you know their secret of success? Do you think it's hamburgers, or their french fries or shakes? None of them, my friends. It is the system that Ray Kroc created. He built a formula on how to run, operate, and cook everything so that they have quality controls and thus ensure success for their business owners. But if you study their strategy further you will learn they are in the real estate business! Please check out the movie or book *The Founder*. And here, my dear friends, we are building your system for a successful life—your Epic Life—and that system will accelerate your progress big time. It has been shown to work for many years, and if you apply it, you will enjoy an amazing life, but it is based on your design. I will give you the system, but you apply it for what you want. If anyone follows the Ray Kroc system for business franchises, do you think they will succeed? Yes, big time. Almost everything in life has a secret for doing things, and many times if you follow the fundamentals, you will experience that too. Thus, for us our focus is building a daily routine for action.

DAILY ROUTINE TO CHANGE YOUR LIFE

For example, here is my daily routine.

Morning (Values—Health and Family): Most days I wake up naturally between 5:00 and 6:30 a.m., sometimes earlier. (I do not use an alarm.) I meditate using a gratitude mantra or just pray with deep faith for my family. I will share some of these techniques with you later in this chapter, but I also drink water with vitamins—recently I have been supplementing with beet powder or lemon, but you may want to explore to find what's best for you—quick exercise (30 minutes), sauna, and/or cold plunge. I read 20 minutes or listen to a book. I also review my goals for the day, and I read my goals for the year and the quarter.

Mid-Morning (Values—Mastery or Service, Career or Business): I work intensely on my daily goals, focusing big time for 90 minutes, up to three cycles per day (one intense routine is equal to 90 minutes). This technique will accelerate your performance and ability to get the job done in ways you will not believe. In each cycle I work diligently for 90 minutes, nonstop. I do up to five cycles when I am under extreme stress to finish big projects. Otherwise, on regular days I just work one to three cycles for 90 minutes per day but devote that intense time to my most important goal of the day. By doing this, you know your energy is devoted to those goals that will propel your life big time. If you study any super-successful CEO, you will learn they protect their time and they focus on what matters to the growth of their company. You, as the CEO of your life, must employ that strategy so that you achieve your goals big time!

Afternoon (Values—Career or Business): Then I catch up on other things I am doing with my team or projects my graduate students are working on with quick texts or emails and have meetings at the university. If you are a student or an employee, I am saying you should work on the most important task very early in the morning, then in the afternoon you attend class or attend meetings. By converting your quiet time of the morning into your opportunity to make big progress in your research or studies, you will accelerate the output of your work. You become more efficient because you do not have interruptions.

Night (Values—Self-Mastery or Service, Family and Friends, Health): I don't structure my evenings as much as my days, but instead align this time with my overall wellness and my priorities with my children. I may spend time with family and friends (FaceTime or quick call), exercise more if I'm training for a triathlon, or spend the time reading and learning. In the evenings, I cook with my youngest daughter, or we go for dinner. At this time, we talk about life and our plans for the summer, or I learn how things are going in her life. This time is for bonding and building a strong foundation.

Now, let's talk about you and how you can build a routine. If this is a new way of thinking for you, start small.

Your Morning Routine (Health, Self-Mastery): You can start small: Give yourself an extra 30 minutes in the morning by waking up earlier. Put yourself in a state of gratitude (see the next section, "A Positive Mindset to Start an Epic Day") and drink water if possible, because your body needs hydration after eight hours of sleep (lemon has vitamin C and helps you put your body in an alkaline pH), and/or read for 20 minutes, or listen to something inspiring, or just give thanks to God/the universe for the gift of a new day. Starting the day with something as little as that, think how many books you can read in a year and how much your state of mind will change—think how you will show up for your children, your partner, or your positive attitude in class. Learn to be grateful for your life; it will make you a more positive and happier person.

Your Day (Health, Friends): Depending on where you are in life—studying, working, or seeking your next phase—seek opportunities to apply some of what we've discussed in this book. If you are working a 9:00 a.m.–5:00 p.m. job, use lunchtime to walk with a colleague or friend, or if you can, just go to the gym or do a yoga class together. This hour will oxygenate your body and mind, and you will come back very energized. It is well known that exercise increases your levels of endorphins—these are neurotransmitters that are produced in your brain, act as a pain reliever, and improve your mood. Friends, something like a simple walk or exercise will improve your physical body and your brain health—you kill two birds with one stone. Think of your goals or listen to your recorded voice. This will increase your burning desire and thus will help you be more productive.

Your Night (Health, Self-Mastery and Giving, Family and Friends): I recommend that you align your evening with your goals—use evening for learning and building strong bonds with people you care about and love. When you build stronger bonds with loved ones, your well-being improves overall. But because you're earlier in your journey, you may need to take some extra time to think harder about those goals, about what you learned during the day, and about how you can move just a little bit closer toward your Epic Life. Then enjoy some exercise, some time with family and friends, and read or watch a documentary about something you're interested in. This small routine is part of your self-mastery. Have the courage to build a routine.

A POSITIVE MINDSET TO START AN EPIC DAY

I will share with you some techniques you can employ to get yourself in a positive state to grow a peaceful, resilient mind and a grateful heart. This is part of your health plan, because a strong, healthy body is not enough to be amazing: We need a mind that is centered, calm, and peaceful, and a heart that is filled with joy. In my experience, these activities have been instrumental in overcoming difficult times, giving me steadiness and trust that everything will be fine.

Positive Affirmations: Here, you want to tell yourself positive things early in the day or even several times a day. Putting positive thoughts in your mind will have an impact on your attitude and how you approach life. A lot of advice will tell you this, but I'm here to tell you it really works: Telling yourself who you are, in a positive tone, with deep conviction, will drastically change your life. Encouraging yourself this way helps you believe that you are destined for greatness and that whatever situation you are facing now, you will overcome. The following are positive affirmations that I say out loud or listen to every day. I shared this list with my children as an example from which to create their own. Here are my Daily Positive Affirmations (I recorded this on my phone and listen to it every day):

DAILY POSITIVE AFFIRMATIONS
I am Divinely Guided
I am Strong
I am Calm
I am Peaceful
I am Sexy and Rich
I am Loved
I am Amazing
I am Brilliant
I am Beautiful
I am Creative
I am Energetic
I am a Genius
I am Love
I am Youthful

I am Healthy
I am Courageous
I am Connected to the Universe
I am Protected by God

For me, listening to these affirmations is super powerful; it helps me stay positive, grateful for my life, and centers my heart and mind. I get out of bed each morning after reading this in a state of happiness and ready to conquer the day.

A State of Gratitude: Here, in this practice of prayer, we want to bring a deep feeling of gratitude within you and then create an alignment of your mind and heart so that your entire system is in sync and ready to have the best day. I want you to have a deep confidence that even if things are difficult right now, you will succeed because you have blessings from God/the universe, and you are not alone because you are supported by higher powers.

Step 1: Gratitude. *Breathe through your nose (slowly) while keeping your hands on your chest.*

- Say "Thank you" with a deep feeling of gratitude for a new day.
- Keep breathing calmly while counting to 10 three times (three sets of 10 breaths).
- After each set, say "Thank you, God (whatever you believe) for ... "
- In a state of gratitude, say "Thank you" with a deep feeling of gratitude. Give thanks for your loved ones, your job, etc.

Step 2: Deep Feeling of Love and Happiness. *Think of special, happy moments in your life.*

- Think of beautiful moments in your life. Feel deep gratitude and joy from these experiences.
- Be thankful for the moments.
- Put your hands on your chest and feel deep love for yourself.
- Enjoy the experience of such beautiful moments and feelings.

Step 3: Goals. *Think of your goals while having deep feelings of joy, love, and happiness (think or plan your move of your ideal life). Give thanks to the universe/God for your goals.*

- Say your goals out loud and say "Thank you!"
- Do this for each of your goals.
- Picture yourself having reached your goals. Remember the movie of your dream life?
- Have a deep feeling that you are divinely guided and protected.

Daily Meditation: There are many ways people can meditate: by breathing, listening to sounds, standing still, chanting, praying, and so on. It is not my goal here to give you all the types of meditations you can employ to help you synchronize your body and mind. Although I always listen to meditations from Wim Hof and/or Sara Raymond, I recommend that you explore books and online resources and videos on guided meditations, find something that feels right for you, and be consistent in listening to it for at least a week. If you dislike the practice, try a different one, perhaps shorter, or a different method, or a new teacher, online or in person or in a book.

Meditation is almost a superpower, practiced by many leaders. I meditate every day. Any of the practices listed above will get your body-mind-heart in a state of happiness and confidence that you will be fine and achieve your Epic Life. You will not regret it—your mind will be at ease, centered, and calm—and your practice will become fundamental to your Epic Life.

COMMITMENT TO CONTINUOUS GROWTH AND LEARNING

During the day, as you drive or cook or clean, listen to a book that will help you learn about areas of your goals that you will need to improve if you want to achieve them (health, fitness, finance, emotional intelligence [EQ], speed reading, improving communications, becoming a better salesperson, etc.). Strive to apply one to three new ideas from those books or podcasts. If you read twelve books per year and apply two new ideas from each, think how much you will grow in a year! You will skyrocket your life!

HEALTH: DIET AND EXERCISE

I am not a nutritionist or a fitness guru, but friends, for you to live an Epic Life your body and mind must be in top shape. In the previous sections we talked meditation and being pumped up, we talked about mood and mental well-being, but now we'll talk about eating well and exercising. Build the best healthy body and mind you can; this will make everything else possible for you, as your health is the greatest treasure you have, please take it serious! Here is my own basic routine:

- Running, cycling, or walking a minimum of 30 minutes a day
- Strength building at least twice a week

A couple of times a year, I train for a marathon or a triathlon, and my routine supercharges my life big time, and I use it to push myself physically. But this basic level of movement is easy to make into a habit that fits into my routine and keeps me in shape and ready to execute my plans.

I urge you to choose a form of physical activity that works for you. It could be yoga, dancing, tennis, weightlifting, running, or cycling. If it helps to set a big goal, sign up and train for a competition. Be physical; build muscles to sustain your body balance. A strong body supports a strong mind, and a strong mind makes a strong person; together they will take you far. And the added benefit is that getting in shape will make you feel more confident (healthier brain), and soon you'll have an energy and magnetism that others will notice.

There's a lot of research that connects exercise to mental health and mood (brain health). When you incorporate physical exercise into your morning routines of gratitude, meditations with breathing exercises, and prayers with faith, you will radiate a positive energy that is exciting to be around. That positive attitude will take you far and will make everyone around you better. If you feel great physically and feel happy mentally, then imagine improving your appearance in the world with nice clothes, a neat haircut, and general good grooming—my friend, you will show up as very attractive. Taking good care of yourself says to others, "I love myself and I take pride in who I am and what I do." These small changes in your daily routines will make a big impact on your overall well-being and performance in school or work or with your family. Stay strong and do not give up. I know you can be a better version of you!

CHAPTER SUMMARY

The Aladdin of the Disney movie does not exist—sorry to burst your bubble. Nobody is going to give your dreams to you; there is no quick fix to most problems. You must do the work day by day over many years. If you believe otherwise, you are fooling yourself. At the end of the day, only you will be the one doing the work to achieve your goals. No one will give you a trophy because you created a blueprint for yourself— you *must go out* and then deliver the work day in and day out for many years. This is how you end up being "lucky."

Alexander the Great's mother, Olympias, used to tell him he was both the son of Zeus and of his real father, King Philip II of Macedonia. Alexander was raised believing he was destined for greatness, and yes, he built the greatest empire of that time and is considered one of the greatest generals of all times. His mother planted the seeds of greatness in him, that he was divinely guided by his father, Zeus!

When we were doing your affirmations, the goal was to put greatness in you and for you to be positive about your day ahead. You build a road map and will work hard for many years, and you will learn to trust that your "failures" contain lessons and make you stronger, and you will learn to trust that you are not alone because you are divinely guided and ultimately will be able to give to others. You know that you are connected—to the universe, God, or whatever higher power you believe in. This helps you stay calm, centered, and peaceful in spite of the difficulties you will face along the path of your Epic Life.

The other piece of "Faith in Action" is having a deep faith in yourself and your vision. As you imagine your ideal life, do it with a deep faith in its truth and know that if your "ideal life" doesn't become reality as you imagine it, something better is waiting for you. This approach helps you let go of the past and look forward with confidence in yourself.

That faith and belief in yourself and the universe will give you inner strength. This is a superpower that nobody can take away from you! It does not matter what is going on; you will know you are not alone, and you will be fine.

If you put the work in, over time you will reap the rewards. The notion of something for nothing is the biggest scam—life is not designed that way! Someone who is selling you something that is very easy is usually trying to take you for a ride. Sometimes your goals will take longer to reach than at other times; other times things do not work out. If things do not work, you may need to adjust your blueprint or action plan. Other times, you will need to educate yourself more on how to be successful in that area. Remember, you will need to evolve to achieve something you never had, and that is the purpose of creating a routine. Building your Epic Life is your responsibility.

CHAPTER ACTIVITIES

ACTIVITY #15. Daily Routines

Time needed: Approximately 20 minutes.

   15a. Create an easy 30-minute morning routine that inspires you
         and gets you ready for an awesome day.

15b. Create a routine for your day. What are your most critical goals for next quarter? Then, build a day routine that will help you target those critical goals.

15c. Evening routine: How would you like your evening routine to look? Which values would you like to focus on in the evening?

15d. Start your morning routine for the next 30 days, then make some minor adjustments and apply it for another 30 days. After your first 30 days, apply your day routine that will accelerate your big goals for the quarter.

15e. After 60 days, integrate your evening routine into your daily life.

15f. At the end of quarter #1, what works well for you? What do you need to improve or change? Apply the lessons you learned to the following quarter.

RECOMMENDATIONS

App

Wim Hof: The Wim Hof Method. Official App, since 2020. A guided technique of breathing, cold exposure, and mental focus to boost your immune system, energy, and clarity when facing stress.

Books

The Power of Now. Eckhart Tolle. New World Library, 1997. A spiritual guide on anchoring yourself in the present and freeing your mind from suffering.

The Miracle Morning. Hal Elrod. Hal Elrod International, 2012. Transform your life before 8:00 a.m. with a powerful and positive morning routine.

The War of Art. Steven Pressfield. Black Irish Entertainment, 2002. A call to action to defeat inner resistance and create with discipline and courage.

Practicing Peace in Times of War. Pema Chödrön. Shambhala, 2007. Buddhist teachings on cultivating inner peace amid external chaos.

Meditations. Marcus Aurelius. 2nd Century; various modern editions (e.g., Penguin Classics, 2006). Stoic reflections from an emperor on virtue, duty, and mental tranquility.

The End of Mental Illness. Daniel G. Amen. Tyndale Refresh, 2020. A comprehensive proposal to heal and prevent mental disorders from a neurological perspective.

The Art of Living. Thich Nhat Hanh. HarperOne, 2017. Buddhist wisdom applied to daily life: presence, compassion, and inner transformation.

What to Say When You Talk to Yourself. Shad Helmstetter. Park Avenue Press, 1986. Explores the power of internal dialogue and how to reprogram your mind with positive affirmations.

Activate Your Full Human Potential. Wim Hof. Kitsune Books, 2022. A natural method for self-healing, energy, and focus to face physical and mental adversity.

The Power of I Am. Joel Osteen. FaithWords, 2016. A spiritual and practical approach to building active faith and hope in the face of life's trials.

The Energy Explosion. Robin Sharma. Audiobook, HarperCollins, 2020. Strategies to regain vitality, focus, and passion for life.

The 5AM Club. Robin Sharma. HarperCollins, 2018. A system for starting your day with discipline, clarity, and personal growth.

The Untethered Soul. Michael A. Singer. New Harbinger Publications, 2007. A journey toward inner freedom through awareness and spiritual surrender.

Biographies

Mother Teresa: A Heart Full of Love. Jean Maalouf. Paulinas, 1996. A life built with simple acts of service and prayer in the midst of suffering.

The Book of Joy. Dalai Lama & Desmond Tutu. Avery, 2016. Conversations on how to find joy amid pain—with humor, compassion, and wisdom.

Peace Is Every Step. Thich Nhat Hanh. Bantam, 1991. Teaches how mindfulness can turn any ordinary moment into an act of peace.

Bonhoeffer: Pastor, Martyr, Prophet, Spy. Eric Metaxas. Thomas Nelson, 2010. The story of spiritual and moral resistance against the Nazi regime.

Way of the Peaceful Warrior. Dan Millman. HJ Kramer, 1980. A semiauto-biographical spiritual novel about inner transformation through body, mind, and spirit.

Movies

Peaceful Warrior. Dir. Victor Salva. Lionsgate, 2006. Inspired by Dan Millman's story, it teaches how presence can transform even the simplest moments.

Into Great Silence. Dir. Philip Gröning. Zeitgeist Films, 2005. A contemplative documentary about the silent lives of Carthusian monks.

The Way. Dir. Emilio Estevez. Filmax, 2010. A father walks the Camino de Santiago in honor of his son and finds emotional healing along the journey.

A Man Called Otto. Dir. Marc Forster. Sony Pictures, 2022. A widowed man's closed-off routine is transformed through simple acts of connection and humanity.

Works of Art

The Garden of Earthly Delights, by Hieronymus Bosch, c. 1490–1510. Prado Museum, Madrid. A triptych representing the soul's spiritual journey from human desire to the transcendent.

The Angelus, by Jean-François Millet, 1857–1859. Musée d'Orsay, Paris. A rural scene symbolizing simple spirituality integrated into daily life.

Las Meninas, by Diego Velázquez, 1656. Prado Museum, Madrid. A masterpiece revealing the symbolic depth hidden in the routines of courtly life.

Daily Bread, by Jean-Baptiste-Siméon Chardin, 18th century. Louvre Museum, Paris. A celebration of domestic ritual and the beauty of the present moment.

10

A Life Well Lived

Your Legacy, Your Gift to the World

*It is not the wealth or power that defines a man, but
his character and the impact he leaves on the world.*
—ALEXANDER THE GREAT OF MACEDONIA

END OF THE GAME

In the end, achieving, doing, and having great "toys" means nothing
if during your time on Earth you did nothing to enhance the lives of
others. As a teenager a book that changed my view was *Jonathan Livingston Seagull* by Richard Bach. It is an inspiring story of a seagull who
just wanted to learn to fly and fly fast. He became the fastest seagull that
ever existed. However, in the process of learning to fly, he learned that
his true purpose in life was not flying but helping other seagulls to learn
to fly and to be more: to be the best they can be and to share with others
the gift that you get by becoming the best you can be. The journey of
achieving was more about becoming spiritual—becoming light! This
chapter is about learning your purpose in this life—that purpose is the
gift given to you by the heavens to share with your brothers and sisters.

In the previous chapter we went in depth about building your blueprint for an epic year, which builds the foundation for an Epic Life. You envisioned a movie of your ideal life. However, do you think an Epic Life must include an epic end? Yes, otherwise it cannot be epic!

How do you see your amazing, beautiful story ending? Imagining this ending is what we are going to do now. We talked about goals + vision + values, with goals often relegated to New Year's resolutions. I want you to envision the end of your life. In our modern culture, talking about death is often viewed fearfully or negatively.

Over two years ago, I played a game with my then girlfriend, which was writing our eulogies. It turned out to be something significant for me—it reshaped my life in many ways. Everything I now choose is much more intentional and meaningful than before. Writing my eulogy was an illuminating experience, because in doing so I saw my life 20 to 30 years from now—ending.

As previously mentioned, death is not viewed as something to talk about in mainstream American culture. In fact, most people in our country have been taught to fear death. The exercise here is for you to examine the kind of person you have been on this beautiful earth—and, better yet, what gift you gave to the world in exchange for having been given the honor to be alive.

THE EULOGY

A eulogy, according to the dictionary, is a speech or piece of writing that praises someone or something. When you wake up from watching the movie at the end of your life, I want you to write your own eulogy. Think about the following points:

- What do you want people to say about you?
- How do you touch the lives of others?

- How do you, by your actions, words, and love, touch your family and friends, community, country, and maybe even the world?

The activities at the end of the chapter will help you find your vision and purpose. Please, go now and do Activities 17–19.

My Vision: I want to bring energy security and knowledge to many countries in the world, so that people in this world can live a better life. *And yes, become the best man that I can be!*

My Purpose: Inspire others to find their gift and bring hope to others.

My Values: Values are a set of rules that determine someone's behavior and help a person make decisions in life. You know when you are near a person with high standards and values. Examples are the following:

- Integrity
- Freedom
- Love
- Knowledge
- Health
- Family and friends
- Persistence

In your movie and eulogy, some common words will show up that can be translated into one to three values that are critical to you. For example, I value freedom a great deal—it is so important to me that it shaped my professional career choice in such a way that I have the freedom to pursue my own curiosity and direction in my career and personal life. In fact, at the age of 23, I asked myself which career I could pursue that would allow me the freedom to do whatever I want without having to be owned by a boss at a company. Guess what? I ended up doing a PhD because being a professor is the closest thing to what I wanted in this regard. Every research project and teaching decision is made based on that premise. And yes, I work on renewable energy because I want people to have opportunities to be the best they can and live their life to the fullest. Friends, my energy corridors and big, bold goals are around energy and hope.

My family and friends are super important to me, as are integrity and health. Learning, acquiring knowledge, is also important to me. A person with values is attractive to me. Individuals with goals and a vision will attract others in many ways, including as a leader. When you have a clear blueprint of your life, you know where you are going and why; it changes everything. This clear direction translates to confidence; a confident person is super attractive. When you have your life in order and are committed to be a better you, others may be inspired to do the same. People will follow you when you put yourself in the driver's seat of your life. Do not be a co-driver, or worse, a passenger, following the dreams of others. This is your own journey—and it must be yours because this is your life. Remember that you deserve an Epic Life, and in return give your very best to this world so the life of the next generation is better because you were here.

A person with direction whose values stand for something and who works toward goals will be a more desirable job candidate and better employee. These types of people help their unit to grow; they help their team; they are good communicators; they know how to solve problems; they give to others; they add value.

Be Proud, Be Excellent, Be Humble, Be Amazing, and Build an Epic Life!

- Be proud, not arrogant.
- Be excellent; push for greatness and never compromise greatness for average performance or mediocrity.
- Be humble and kind to others, but never lower your standards or be a pushover, a nice person with no spine. Never let anyone disrespect you or confuse your humility for a sucker. If necessary,

defend who you are and those you love. Be willing to take a stand and say *no!*

- Be amazing and be the best version of you today; be you and be a blessing to the world.
- Be you, be brave, and dare to build an Epic Life, your Epic Life, one that touches many people; one that brings light and love to humanity.

By aggressively pursuing your blueprint, you will build a life well-lived—an Epic Life! This book has guided you through a long journey. You've put in a lot of work. Having a blueprint for an Epic Life can make you feel proud! You know with certainty that your life will be amazing and that you are not alone, that you are connected to the universe/God.

> *No matter what you look at, if you look at it closely*
> *enough, you are involved in the entire universe.*
> —MICHAEL FARADAY

It's important to stay grounded. Be confident, but not arrogant. Arrogance is usually a sign that a person is covering up for something lacking inside of them. It can be a sign of insecurity, a lack of self-confidence—instead, be like Mark Manson who in his amazing books said, "Don't give a fuck—be genuinely you." You have a detailed blueprint, a vision for your life and values, and even a eulogy. You, my friend, know where you are going, and do you know why? You have brought faith/hope inside your body, in your mind, and you have learned to connect with a higher consciousness. You have a super-powerful source of energy behind you, so for all that you have written, all that you will achieve for yourself, your family, and all of us, be proud! You were given life by your parents, but the person you became from the inside out is a gift to the world.

As you push forward once again (remember, the first time was to win the fertilization race!), do it at an exceptional level. Move forward at the level at which an elite athlete or world-renowned scientist would, with class, dignity, and in pursuit of greatness. Some days will be rough, but you just need to keep climbing!

As you proudly pursue greatness and achieve your big, audacious goals, be happy, be proud, and above all, be humble! Humility is a sign of greatness. A highly dignified individual who is an elite performer, one who is proud and humble, is also approachable and can serve as a great role model to a young person looking for guidance or just some encouragement—you can do it! Thank you for taking this journey with me.

CHAPTER SUMMARY

This final chapter is a heartfelt reflection on what truly matters at the end of life's journey. It's not about wealth, fame, or the number of "toys" you've collected. It's about your legacy—the love you gave, the light you shared, and the lives you touched. I've always believed that an Epic Life deserves an epic ending. That's why I invite you here to look ahead and ask yourself: How do I want to be remembered? What impact do I want to leave on this beautiful Earth?

I share with you one of the most transformative exercises I've ever done—writing my own eulogy. Yes, really. Imagining my last day gave me clarity about how I want to live every day. And now I challenge you to do the same: to write the final scene of your life story, to make sure the way you live today leads to the legacy you dream of.

In this chapter, I guide you through defining your vision, your purpose, and your core values. Because once you know who you are and where you're going, you move through life with more confidence and grace. I show you how my own values—freedom, love, knowledge, health, integrity—have guided me through difficult decisions. And I invite you to identify the values that light your path, so you can live not by reaction but by creation.

A well-lived life is not about perfection. It's about intention, generosity, and purpose. You don't have to be a movie hero—you just have to become someone who inspires others with your actions. If, when your time comes, you can look back with peace—knowing you gave your best, loved deeply, and served with heart—then my friend . . . you truly lived an Epic Life.

Thank you for walking this journey with me. Now it's your turn to inspire the world—with the best version of you.

CHAPTER ACTIVITIES

ACTIVITY #16. Legacy

Time needed: Approximately 20–30 minutes. Note: This activity is critical as it will help to identify your life vision, values, and purpose. So please, as in building your big, bold life, be in a place where you feel relaxed and comfortable without any interruptions or external noise. Play a calm, peaceful background song if you wish. You must be in the best possible state to visualize this stage of your life.

16a. *The End: Play a Movie in Your Mind of the End of Your Life.* Think about being eulogized. What do you want people to say about your life? What do you hope your existing or future children will say? As you can see, goals have a lot to do with leaving a legacy. To do this, listen to beautiful, soft music that will help you relax and be calm. Then close your eyes. Think of your last moments on this earth and imagine whom you see near you (e.g., your partner, your best friend from childhood, your kids, siblings, people whose lives you touched, people that touched your life, etc.). Please take the time to see what you say to them. Then imagine a funeral service with people singing songs. What songs do you hear? What stories are being shared about you—can you recall a funny story that can bring laughter? What is your close friend saying about you? Your partner, if you have one, is saying what? See colors, hear songs, even imagine the altar. How many people did you touch because of your contributions and your love for them, for humanity, or by just being you? See the place where people are gathering, then see the cars moving with your children, grandchildren, your colleagues (who is there?), and what are people saying about you? Then imagine the person closest to you, who now comes and stands tall and dignified, the person who wrote your eulogy. Try to remember everything that is said and the final good-bye. The movie must have motion, sounds, colors, and also show people's faces. See the details of that end of journey goodbye.

ACTIVITY #17. Eulogy

Time needed: Approximately 30–60 minutes for this.

17a. *The End: Write Your Eulogy.* If your eulogy is 1 to 10 pages, do not worry about it. Once you have finished, read it again and underline one sentence that you think conveys your vision in this life.

ACTIVITY #18. Vision

Time needed: Approximately 10 minutes.

18a. What is your vision in this life? Write a sentence from your eulogy that represents your life vision.

The key here is that you see the end to help you establish a clear purpose for your life. This is especially important as you will see that your long-term goals for 10 years and beyond align with your vision. Ideally you want your mid-term goals of five years or so to be moving in that direction, but do not worry about this.

Your objective is to have a clear direction and a clear purpose about who you are. In fact, from this exercise, you can extract a lot of information about your long-term goals, your life vision, and your values.

ACTIVITY #19. Purpose

Time needed: Approximately 10 minutes.

19a. What is your purpose in life? Write a sentence for your purpose in this life.

ACTIVITY #20. Values

Time needed: Approximately 10 minutes.

20a. Write 3–5 values. What do you value?

BOOK ACTIVITIES

The best way to predict your future is to create it.
—ABRAHAM LINCOLN

1. Identify 3–5 quotes in this book that touched you. Why?
2. For each quote you identified, find further information about the author and historical time. What did you learn and how will you apply it to your current state in life?
3. Rewrite your life vision, purpose, and values.
4. Rewrite and modify, if necessary, your goals for Year 1. Which is your epic goal of the year? Why?
5. Rewrite and modify your goals for 3–5 years (mid-term goals) and your long-term goals.

RECOMMENDATIONS

Books

The Art of Happiness. Dalai Lama & Howard Cutler. Riverhead Books, 1998. A dialogue between science and Tibetan wisdom on how to build a life grounded in compassion, joy, and purpose.

Tuesdays with Morrie. Mitch Albom. Doubleday, 1997. Heartfelt conversations between a dying professor and his student about the values that truly matter at the end of life.

Man's Search for Meaning. Viktor E. Frankl. Beacon Press, 1946. A profound reflection on finding meaning even in the most painful circumstances—essential to understanding the power of legacy.

Legacy. James Kerr. Constable, 2013. Leadership, humility, and purpose lessons from the All Blacks rugby team—how to build a lasting culture of values.

The Top Five Regrets of the Dying. Bronnie Ware. Hay House, 2011. A palliative care nurse shares the most common end-of-life confessions. A call to live authentically starting today.

Love Yourself Like Your Life Depends on It. Kamal Ravikant, 2012. A book about learning to love oneself, it gives meditations and useful exercises.

Biographies

Reason for Hope. Jane Goodall. Warner Books, 1999. Beyond science, Goodall conveys a legacy of hope, respect for life, and harmony with nature.

Frederick Douglass: Prophet of Freedom. David W. Blight. Simon & Schuster, 2018. The life of a former slave who became one of the greatest advocates for freedom and human dignity.

Long Walk to Freedom. Nelson Mandela. Little, Brown and Company, 1994. The autobiography of a leader whose struggle and forgiveness laid the foundation for a new nation.

Rachel Carson: Witness for Nature. Linda Lear. Mariner Books, 1997. A pioneer of modern environmentalism whose legacy reshaped how we understand and protect the Earth.

The Conscientious Objector. Desmond Doss. Documentary, 2004. The true story of a soldier who saved over 70 lives in WWII without using a weapon. Inspired the film Hacksaw Ridge.

Movies

The Bucket List. Dir. Rob Reiner. Warner Bros., 2007. Two terminally ill men go on a journey to fulfill their dreams before they die. Reflective and moving.

Schindler's List. Dir. Steven Spielberg. Universal Pictures, 1993. The true story of a businessman who saved over a thousand Jews during the Holocaust—a legacy of humanity in the face of horror.

Coco. Dir. Lee Unkrich. Pixar/Disney, 2017. An animated film that celebrates family memory and the power of legacy across generations.

Life Itself. Dir. Dan Fogelman. Amazon Studios, 2014. An interwoven story showing how every life, with its highs and lows, leaves a mark on others.

Pay It Forward. Dir. Mimi Leder. Warner Bros., 2000. A young boy creates a chain of kindness that transforms his community. The power of good as a lasting inheritance.

Bicentennial Man. Dir. Chris Columbus. Columbia Tristar Film Distributors International (1999). A science-comedy-drama film with Robin Williams about a journey of a robot that becomes human.

Works of Art

The Tree of Life, by Gustav Klimt, 1905. Museum of Applied Arts, Vienna. Represents the connection between generations, spiritual growth, and the continuous flow of human existence.

La Pietà, by Michelangelo, 1499. St. Peter's Basilica, Vatican City. A sculpture capturing sorrow, compassion, and eternal love between mother and son—a universal spiritual legacy.

The Thinker, by Auguste Rodin, 1880. Rodin Museum, Paris. Symbolizes human contemplation about action, purpose, and one's impact on the world.

La Madre, by Oswaldo Guayasamín, 20th century. Guayasamín Foundation, Quito. Expresses maternal suffering and tenderness as the foundation of resistance, humanity, and the continuity of life.

Martin Luther King Jr. Memorial. Washington, D.C. Inaugurated 2011. A monumental sculpture that immortalizes his message: "Darkness cannot drive out darkness; only light can do that."

Epilogue

The first and greatest victory is to conquer yourself.
—PLATO

Your attitude plays a big role in unleashing the greatness within you, this is the Epic of Your Life, the hero's journey. Carrying yourself with dignity serves as an inspiration and a model for others. As you culminate this journey with me, keep in mind that the blueprint you created is there for you as you continue your journey to greatness. You can adjust it and change it over time so it will fit into the current events in your life and future.

To support this journey, read the recommended books, movies, podcasts, attend workshops, be good to yourself physically, mentally, and spiritually—learn to feel a deep love for yourself because then you can give it to others. Doing these things will help you create a legacy that goes beyond your work since you will have served as an inspiration to others along the way. If you live your life this way, the lives of others will be more meaningful because you were here. You will have touched their lives. This is how a true giant, an elite human being, closes the final chapter of a life well lived, a life filled with true passion, a life of meaning, and a life that supported and inspired many others. In the end, that life was a true gift of love to humanity!

The more people you help become exceptional, the more our human race evolves toward a level of consciousness and understanding of our universe. So long and see you again, my dear friends!

With love and respect,

Luciano

Building Your Epic Life:
Your Journey, Your Way, Your Masterpiece

About the Author

LUCIANO CASTILLO is a nationally recognized advocate for mentoring, diversity, and innovation in STEM education. His journey began in the 1990s at the State University of New York at Buffalo, where he studied science and engineering. Since then, he has built a legacy of inclusive leadership, community engagement, and academic excellence, working with organizations such as the Society of Hispanic Engineers and the National Society of Black Engineers to create mentorship programs for youth and students. Currently the Kenninger Professor of Renewable Energy and Power Systems in the School of Mechanical Engineering at Purdue University, Castillo founded the Trailblazers in Engineering program, which supports doctoral and postdoctoral scholars in their transition to academic careers. Passionate about mentorship, he has led several summer research institutes focused on renewable energy and medicine, serving students, K–12 educators, and college faculty.